Traditional
Island Knitting

Traditional Island Knitting

including
Aran, Channel Isles, Fair Isle,
Falkland Isles, Iceland and Shetland

Pam Dawson

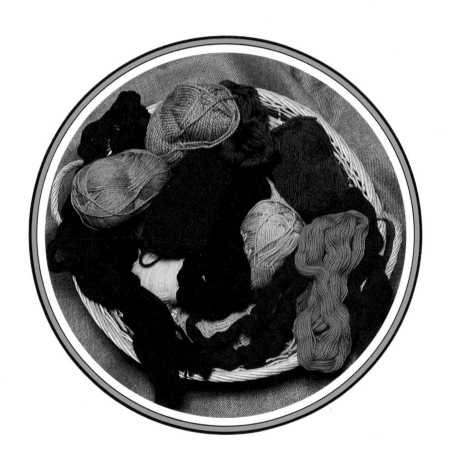

GUILD PUBLISHING
LONDON

First published in Great Britain 1988

This editon published 1988 by
Guild Publishing by arrangement with

Search Press Ltd,
Wellwood, North Farm Road,
Tunbridge Wells, Kent, TN2 3DR.

Written and edited by Pam Dawson
Photography, Search Press Studios
Technical illustrations, Jan Messent
Designer, Julie Wood
Assistant Editor, Rosalind Dace
Fair Isle charts, Marilyn Clark

Typeset by Scribe Design, 123 Watling Street, Gillingham, Kent
Printed in Spain by Elkar S. Coop, Bilbao 12

Contents

Introduction

The craft of knitting has evolved over very many centuries and although it is impossible to say exactly where, and when it began, small fragments of interlocked fabric discovered during various periods of archaeological excavation seem to indicate that some form of knitting originated in Arabia. The nomad people of these regions did much to encourage the development of the craft and, quite early in its history, had produced a knitting frame very similar to the knitting bobbin used by children today.

From Arabia, different aspects of the craft eventually spread throughout the known world. In the early eighth century the Arabs began a policy of territorial expansion and gained control of part of the Iberian Peninsula. By the eleventh century, Spain had become the centre of the technique of knitting with needles, which we know today as hand-knitting. Knowledge of the craft spread rapidly to the rest of Europe and as knitting was closely linked with religion during this time, many of the finest examples were intended as church vestments and furnishings, see opposite page.

No-one can be certain when knitting first appeared in Britain but, once introduced, it quickly became established and poverty-striken families were quick to grasp the opportunity of earning an income in their own homes. By the thirteenth century the woollen industry, including the hand-spinning and dyeing of yarn, the weaving of cloth and knitting, had become one of the most profitable in our entire history. This trade was so important that many of the laws and customs of our country were established during this period to protect it—the first introduction of an export tax on the profitable commodity; a system of patrolling the seas with convoys of ships to overcome the problem of piracy and the use of a sack of wool as part of our parliamentary regalia, to remind all members of the source of the wealth of the country.

By the late fifteenth century, knitting had become associated with fashionable wearing apparel and such items as stockings, gloves, caps and shirts were produced in vast quantities. Examples of felted woollen caps of the early Tudor period are to be seen in the Victoria and Albert Museum in London and an Act of Parliament passed during the reign of Henry VII in 1488 relates to knitted caps. Glimpses of the general interest in knitting also appear casually in household accounts of the time, and it is obvious that the craft had been absorbed into the routine of everyday life.

It is not until the dawning of the Elizabethan age, however, that knitting became not just a practical, everyday craft but a creative and beautiful art form. The foundation of Knitting Guilds during this period brought together, for the first time, the colour appreciation and creative talent of the artist with the technical skill of the artisan. Men had always dominated the craft and although women and children had by now mastered the skill to add to meagre incomes, and schools had even been established to teach knitting, only men and boys were admitted to the Guilds. For a period of about six years an apprentice learned the various techniques, both at home and abroad, and his subsequent examination entailed knitting a shirt, a cap, a pair of stockings and a carpet, or wall-hanging.

During the reign of Elizabeth I, hand-knitted silk stockings became the vogue and it was during this period that the Reverend William Lee invented the first knitting frame capable of producing machine-made stockings. As these quickly replaced the coarser hand-knitted versions, the hosiery trade in and around London was formed. William Lee died in France some time after 1611, before realizing the profound influence his invention would eventually have on the knitting industry. The ancient craft of knitting can thus lay claim to being the forerunner of modern technology, long before the start of the industrial revolution.

With the advent of machine-knitting the old skills declined in most areas but the seventeenth and eighteenth centuries found them firmly established among the famous hand-knitters of the Yorkshire dales. Men, women and children knitted, singing special songs as they clicked away—the faster the rhythm the quicker they knitted. The invaluable knowledge of that period was never written down, but was passed from one generation to another by word of mouth. The craft barely survived during the nineteenth century, but a succession of wars requiring socks and Balaclava helmets for the troops, and the introduction of the popular 'cardigan' by the Earl of Cardigan, brought industry and some small profit to the inventive knitters of the dales.

During the comparatively peaceful times of the middle 1830's the first women's magazines appeared and these were to revolutionize the hand-knitting industry. Knitting soon gained enormous popularity, not as a necessary means of survival but as an interesting and therapeutic hobby. The oldest book in my library, entitled 'The Ladies' Knitting and Netting Book', First Series, is dated 1839. It is a fourth edition, which gives some indication as to its total sales. By

The Buxtehude altar piece, popularly called 'The Knitting Madonna'
was painted by Meister Bertram of Minden, Germany, circa 1400.
The Virgin Mary is shown using a set of four needles to knit the
stitches around the neck of a garment.

modern standards it is crude; unillustrated, and with scant guidance about yarn, needle size and tension. A later book, 'The Lady's Knitting Book', first published in 1884, is also unillustrated and brief headings give little indication of the type of garment which will be produced. On one page a previous owner has found and corrected in ink an error in the instructions for knitting 'Spider stitch'—so mistakes due to human error happened even then!

Today we take full-colour illustrations of superb designs, row-by-row instructions, exact details of qualities and quantities, and correct tension for granted. It is also doubtful whether anything new can now be added to the wealth of technical knowledge, or the variety of stitches and complexities of patterns available to the avid hand-knitter. What does emerge from this welter of information is that however much fashions may come and go, traditional garments remain consistently popular. Rib patterns, cable variations, three-dimensional textures such as bobbles and coloured techniques all exist in knitting traditions throughout the world. What gives a distinctly regional influence to these techniques, however, is the way in which they have been combined in the past, and the type of yarn which has been used to produce different fabrics. Rib and cable patterns have become synonymous with fishermens' garments in almost every fishing port around the entire coastline of the British Isles. The traditional guernsey has a dropped shoulder-line and square armholes and is knitted in flat, brocade-like patterns. The more complex, three-dimensional texture of authentic Aran patterns produce garments which are instantly recognizable. The coloured patterns of the Shetland Isles, particularly Fair Isle, have been adapted as far afield as Iceland and the Falkland Isles. Shetland also continued to produce gossamer lace knitting of exquisite beauty and the traditional wedding ring shawl is unique.

In writing this book, it is my sincere hope that you will gain a new insight into the old and honourable craft of knitting.

Pam Dawson

Fisherman knitting

*This unknown lifeboatman is wearing a fisherman sweater
under his lifejacket. Wives and girlfriends knitted these practical
garments for their menfolk to protect them from harsh
weather conditions and stormy seas.*

Fisherman knitting

Rib patterns cannot justifiably be attributed to any specific region of knitting, as they are universal to all forms of the craft. Travelling stitches are also used in many different techniques, but as they can be used to form miniature cables they play their part in fishermens' designs. True cable patterns, however, are supposed to represent different types of ropes and sailors' knots so they can be used to classify the overall category of fishermens' knitting.

A 'gansey' is the traditional name given to the hard-wearing, practical garment originally knitted in every fishing community around the coast of the British Isles and in many other fishing areas. The name is derived from the Channel Island of Guernsey, but the style of garment produced in this particular island does differ slightly from the typical fishermens' garment of the mainland.

Because of the similarity in the design and name of this type of garment, wherever possible historians prefer to list authentic stitch patterns under their region of origin. Thus we have the Polperro guernsey, or gansey, from Cornwall—locally called a 'knit-frock'; the Whitby gansey from Yorkshire; the Sheringham gansey from Norfolk and the Mussel-burgh gansey from Scotland, to name but a few. Even when a stitch pattern can be identified as coming from a particular region, however, it is almost impossible to say where it may have originated, as fishermen and their womenfolk sailed with the fishing fleets, visiting many ports in their travels. Stitch patterns were traded and constantly added to on these journeys but local folklore would have us believe that any fisherman could be recognized in his home port by the patterns on his gansey. Legends apart, it is true to say that wherever fishermen were located to harvest the riches of the sea, knitting would also be closely interwoven into the community.

The shape and fabric of an authentic fisherman gansey are the two characteristics which identify it, as everything about it was intended to be both practical and hard-wearing. It was square-shaped, with a dropped shoulder line, knitted completely in the round, with the sleeve stitches picked up around the armholes and knitted downwards. For practical purposes the sleeves were usually quite short, to avoid wringing wet cuffs. The yoke, or section of the gansey which covered the chest, was the most heavily-patterned part of the garment as a protection against the biting winds. Provision would have been made for underarm gussets to allow freedom of movement. To give the knitter a point of reference for the position of the gussets and the yoke patterns, a purl stitch would have been worked at each side as a mock seam stitch to indicate the position of the side seams. Thrifty knitters would also often cast on the welt and cast off the cuffs with double wool—it may have looked bulky but added considerably to the life of the gansey.

Although a gansey would not now be considered purely as a working garment, it was part of a whole way of life for almost one hundred and fifty years in the tiny fishing communities. Men, women and children were all adept at knitting and women were also involved in the spinning of the wool by hand. Although there were periods when every available pair of hands was needed to cope with fishing activities, there were also depressingly quiet times, and idle hands were not encouraged. Knitting was an occupation which suited everybody, although with the passing of the years and the introduction of the spinning-jenny at the end of the eighteenth century, hand spinners were not needed and women and children looked to the actual knitting as a means of earning a livelihood. Nimble fingers were needed to cope with the more intricate patterns, and simple sections such as the ribs on the welt and cuffs were not too difficult for tiny fingers.

In the old communities a working gansey was worn, and repaired, or often re-knitted where it was badly worn, until it almost dropped to pieces. Most men had a Sunday-best gansey, however, which was worn to church, or when having photographs taken by new-fangled inventions, when courting, or just plain visiting. A bride-to-be undertook the knitting of a special bridal shirt for her intended to wear on their wedding day. This would be a labour of love, intricately fashioned and patterned to prove her industry to her fiancé's family and incorporating little, secret details, such as his initials woven into the pattern, to prove her love for him.

Today's traditional ganseys will no doubt be knitted with just as much care, but with a little less effort than in times long gone. To help you recapture something of the past, this section on fisherman knitting has been planned to include step-by-step methods of working some of the traditional stitch patterns. It then goes on to give clear and concise instructions for up-to-date versions of fishermen's designs, using modern yarns which are readily available. Like their historical counterparts, these ganseys are both practical and timeless.

Rib, cable and travelling patterns

Rib patterns play a very important role in knitting as their close texture has a very neat appearance and allows the fabric to expand without stretching it out of shape. This elasticity makes them particularly suitable for such areas as welts and cuffs, but rib variations are also ideal as all-over stitch patterns.

Cable and travelling patterns are used extensively in fishermen's designs and are very simple to work.

To work rib stitches

All rib patterns are based on knitting, and then purling, a given number of stitches in a row. In the finer ribs, such as single or double, the knit stitches appear to close over the purl stitches when the fabric is unstretched. All rib patterns form reversible fabrics.

The only point to remember when working rib patterns is that the position of the yarn must be altered each time you change stitches. If you attempt to carry it across the top of the right hand needle, you will be making an additional stitch. This also applies to all textured patterns which incorporate knitting and purling in the same row, with the exception of lace patterns which may require decorative increases.

To work in rib, when changing from a purl to a knit stitch, take the yarn *back* between the two needles so that it is in the correct position to knit the next stitch. When changing from a knit to a purl stitch, bring the yarn *forward* between the two needles so that it is in the correct position ready to purl the next stitch, (see Fig 1).

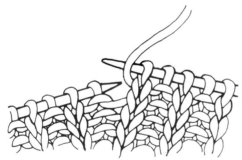

fig 1 changing from a knit to a purl stitch

To work cable stitches

Cable patterns are based on a number of stitches which are moved from one position to another as the row is being worked. These stitches can vary in number, but the complete cable twist should not exceed more than sixteen stitches, or the fabric will be pulled out of shape. The first set of stitches of the cable pattern can either be moved behind, or in front of the next set of stitches in the row, to form twisted ropes. These twisted stitches are usually worked in stocking stitch. To ensure that they show up against the background, stitches on either side of the cable are worked in reversed stocking stitch, or moss stitch. To work these stitches a special cable needle is required to hold the stitches being moved until the twist is completed. This needle is very short and pointed at both ends.

To twist the stitches from right to left, work in pattern until the position for the cable is reached. Place the given number of stitches on to a cable needle and hold this needle at the *front* of the work, knit the required number of stitches needed to complete the cable from the left hand needle in the usual way, then knit the stitches from the cable needle, (see Fig 2).

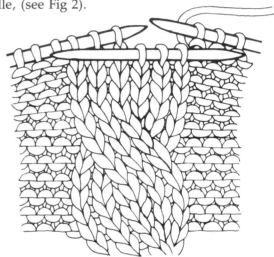

fig 2 twisting stitches from right to left

To twist the stitches from left to right, work in pattern until the position for the cable is reached. Place the given number of stitches on to a cable needle and hold this needle at the *back* of the work, knit the required number of stitches needed to complete the cable from the left hand needle in the usual way, then knit the stitches from the cable needle, (see Fig 3).

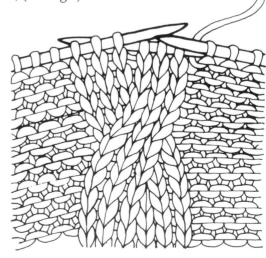

fig 3 twisting stitches from left to right

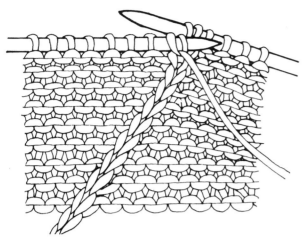

fig 4 *moving one stitch to the right*

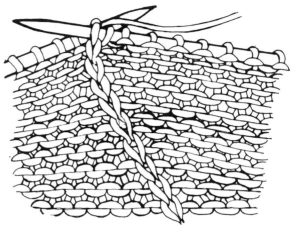

fig 5 *moving one stitch to the left*

To work travelling stitches

A single stitch can be transferred from one position to the next, or two stitches can be twisted round each other as a row is being worked, without the aid of a cable needle.

Single stitches can be moved on every alternate row so that they travel across the surface of the fabric to form lattice patterns, or they can be used to outline areas of contrasting patterns. Two stitches twisted round each other form miniature cables and are a most decorative way of dividing panels of contrasting patterns. In both these methods, the travelling stitches are always worked to show as knit stitches on the right side of the fabric and they show up best against a background of reversed stocking stitch.

To move one knit stitch to the right against a purl background, work until the position for the travelling stitch is reached. Knit into the front of the second stitch on the left hand needle, then purl into the front of the first stitch, dropping both stitches off the needle together, (see Fig 4). When working the following row, remember that the sequence of the stitches has been altered.

To move one knit stitch to the left against a purl background, work until the position for the travelling stitch is reached. Purl into the *back* of the second stitch on the left hand needle, then knit into the front of the first stitch, dropping both stitches off the needle together, (see Fig 5). When working the following row, remember that the sequence of the stitches has been altered.

To twist two knit stitches to the right against a purl background, work until the position for the twisted stitches is reached. Pass the right hand needle across in front of the first stitch on the left hand needle and knit into the front loop of the second stitch, then go back and knit the first stitch in the usual way, dropping both stitches off the needle together, (see Fig 6).

To twist two knit stitches to the left against a purl background, work until the position for the twisted stitches is reached. Pass the right hand needle behind the first stitch on the left hand needle and knit into the *back* loop of the second stitch, then go back and knit the first stitch in the usual way, dropping both stitches off the needle together, (see Fig 7).

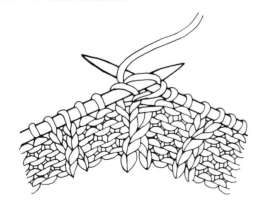

fig 6 *twisting two knit stitches to the right*

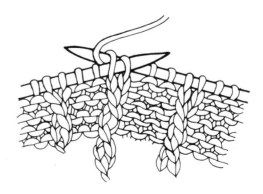

fig 7 *twisting two knit stitches to the left*

Fisherman rib sweater

This chunky sweater is worked in authentic fisherman's rib and is suitable for a man or a woman. The fabric is warm, but lightweight, making it ideal for all outdoor activities.

Measurements

To fit 38 – 40[42 – 44]in/97 – 102[107 – 112]cm bust/chest very loosely
Actual measurements, 45½[49]in/ 116[124]cm
Length to shoulders, 27[27½]in/ 69[70]cm, adjustable
Sleeve seam, 19½[20]in/50[51]cm, adjustable
The figures in [] refer to the 42 – 44/107 – 112cm size only

Materials

21[22] × 50g balls of Emu Folklore
One pair No 7/4½mm needles
One pair No 5/5½mm needles
The quantities of yarn given are based on average requirements and are approximate

Tension

18 sts and 32 rows to 4in/10cm over patt worked on No 5/5½mm needles

Note

Fisherman's rib is formed by knitting into the stitch below the next stitch on the left hand needle, letting both stitches drop off the needle together and is abbreviated as 'K1B'.

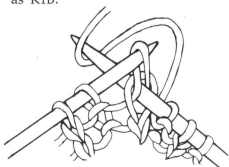

knitting fisherman's rib

Back

With No 7/4½mm needles cast on 103[111] sts.
1st row (Rs) K1, *P1, K1, rep from * to end.
2nd row P1, *K1, P1, rep from * to end.
Rep these 2 rows for 3in/8cm, ending with a 2nd row.
Change to No 5/5½mm needles.
Commence fisherman's rib patt.
1st row (Rs) K to end.
2nd row K1, *K1B (see Note), P1, rep from * to last 2 sts, K1B, K1.
These 2 rows form the patt. Cont in patt until back measures 27[27½]in/69[70]cm from beg, or required length to shoulder, ending with a Ws row.
Cast off loosely.

Front

Work as given for back until front measures 24[24½]in/61[62]cm from beg, or required length to shoulder less 3in/7.5cm, ending with a Ws row.

Shape neck

Next row K44[47] sts, turn and leave rem sts on a spare needle.
Complete left shoulder first.
Dec one st at neck edge on every row until 33[35] sts rem.
Cont without shaping until front measures same as back to shoulder, ending with a Ws row.
Cast off loosely.
With Rs of work facing, sl first 15[17] sts from spare needle on to a holder and leave for centre front neck, rejoin yarn to next st and K44[47] sts.
Complete right shoulder to match left shoulder, reversing shaping.

Sleeves

With No 7/4½mm needles cast on 45[49] sts.
Work 3in/8cm rib as given for back, ending with a 2nd row.
Change to No 5/5½mm needles.
Work in fisherman's rib patt as given for back, inc one st at each end of 3rd and every foll 4th row until there are 97[103] sts.
Cont without shaping until sleeve

measures 19½[20]in/50[51]cm from beg, or required length, ending with a Ws row.
Cast off loosely.

Neckband

Join right shoulder seam.
With Rs of work facing and No 7/4½mm needles, rejoin yarn and pick up and K28[29] sts down left side of front neck, K across front neck sts on holder, pick up and K28[29] sts up right side of front neck and pick up and K across 38[42] back neck sts. 109[117] sts.
Work 3½in/9cm rib as given for beg of back.
Cast off loosely in rib.

To make up

Do not press.
Join left shoulder and neckband seam. Fold neckband in half to Ws and sl st down.
Fold sleeves in half lengthways and, placing fold to shoulder seam, sew in sleeves.
Join side and sleeve seams.

Opposite: A sweater in authentic fisherman's rib.
Designed by Jan Bird.

Pattern pieces

21[23]cm

back and front

69[70]cm

58[62]cm

8cm

54[57]cm

sleeves

50[51]cm

8cm

Jersey in trellis pattern

This jersey features an interesting travelling stitch pattern, which is worked without the use of a cable needle.
The easy-fitting shape has set in sleeves and a round neckline.

Measurements

To fit 30 – 32[34 – 36:38 – 40]in/76 – 81[86 – 91:97 – 102]cm bust
Actual measurements, 36½[39¾:43]in/93[101:109]cm
Length to shoulders, 23½[24½:25¼]in/60[62:64]cm
Sleeve seam, 19[19¼:19¾]in/-48[49:50]cm
The figures in [] refer to the 34 – 36/86 – 91 and 38 – 40in/97 – 102cm sizes respectively

Materials

10[11:12] × 50g balls of Wendy Shetland Double Knitting
One pair No 10/3¼mm needles
One pair No 8/4mm needles
The quantities of yarn given are based on average requirements and are approximate

Tension

25 sts and 30 rows to 4in/10cm over patt worked on No 8/4mm needles

Back

With No 10/3¼mm needles cast on 106[110:114] sts and work 2½in/6cm K1, P1 rib.
Next row (inc row) Rib 7[2:4] sts, *inc in next st, rib 9[6:4] sts, rep from * 8[14:20] times, inc in next st, rib 8[2:4] sts. 116[126:136] sts.

*Opposite: A simple style with round neckline and set-in sleeves, worked in a Shetland yarn. The jersey is criss-crossed with lines of travelling stitches to form an all-over lattice pattern.
Designed by Bea Noble.*

Change to No 8/4mm needles and commence patt.
1st row (Rs) P6, *K into front of 2nd st on left hand needle, then P into front of first st and slip both sts off needle tog — abbreviated as Tw1R —, P into back of 2nd st on left hand needle, then K into front of first st and slip both sts off needle tog — abbreviated as Tw1L —, P6, rep from * to end.
2nd row K6, *P1, K2, P1, K6, rep from * to end.
3rd row P5, *Tw1R, P2, Tw1L, P4, rep from * to last st, P1.
4th row K5, *P1, K4, P1, K4, rep from * to last st, K1.
5th row P4, *Tw1R, P4, Tw1L, P2, rep from * to last 2 sts, P2.
6th row K4, *P1, K6, P1, K2, rep from * to last 2 sts, K2.
7th row P3, *Tw1R, P6, Tw1L, rep from * to last 3 sts, P3.
8th row K2, *P2, K8, rep from * to last 4 sts, P2, K2.
9th row P2, *K next 2 sts tog tbl, then K into back of first st again and slip both sts off needle tog — abbreviated as Sp2 —, P8, rep from * to last 4 sts, Sp2, P2.
10th row As 8th row.
Rep last 2 rows twice more.
15th row P3, *Tw1L, P6, Tw1R, rep from * to last 3 sts, P3.
16th row As 6th row.
17th row P4, *Tw1L, P4, Tw1R, P2, rep from * to last 2 sts, P2.
18th row As 4th row.
19th row P5, *Tw1L, P2, Tw1R, P4, rep from * to last st, P1.
20th row As 2nd row.
21st row P6, *Tw1L, Tw1R, P6, rep from * to end.
22nd row K7, *P2, K8, rep from * to last 9 sts, P2, K7.
23rd row P7, *Sp2, P8, rep from * to last 9 sts, Sp2, P7.
24th row As 22nd row.
Rep last 2 rows twice more.
These 28 rows form patt and are rep throughout.
Cont in patt without shaping until back measures 16[16½:17]in/41[42:43]cm from beg, ending with a Ws row.

Shape armholes

Keeping patt correct, cast off 4 sts at beg of next 2 rows. Dec one st at each end of next and every foll alt row until 84[94:104] sts rem.
Cont without shaping until back measures 23½[24½:25¼]in/60[62:64]cm from beg, ending with a Ws row.

Shape shoulders

Keeping patt correct, cast off 10[12:14] sts at beg of next 4 rows.
Cast off rem 44[46:48] sts fairly loosely for centre back neck.

Front

Work as given for back until front measures 20½[21¼:22]in/52[54:56]cm from beg, ending with a Ws row.

Shape front neck

Next row Patt 37[41:45] sts, turn and complete this side first, leaving rem sts on holder or spare needle.
**Keeping patt correct, dec one st at neck edge on every row until 20[24:28] sts rem. Cont without shaping until front measures same as back to shoulder, ending at armhole edge.

Shape shoulder

Keeping patt correct, cast off at beg of next and foll alt row 10[12:14] sts twice.
With Rs of work facing, rejoin yarn to rem sts, cast off first 10[12:14] sts for centre front neck, patt to end of row.
Complete to match first side from ** to end.

Sleeves

With No 10/3¼mm needles cast on 52 sts and work 2¾in/7cm K1, P1 rib.
Next row (inc row) Rib 6, *inc in next st, rib 2, rep from * 12 times more, inc in next st, rib 6. 66 sts.
Change to No 8/4mm needles.
Cont in patt as given for back, *at the same time* inc one st at each end of every foll 10th[8th:6th] row until there are 74[84:94] sts, working extra sts into patt at each side.
Cont without shaping until sleeve

Pattern pieces

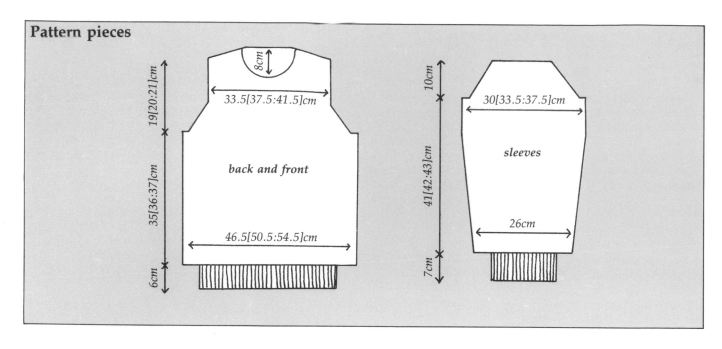

back and front

8cm

33.5[37.5:41.5]cm

19[20:21]cm

35[36:37]cm

6cm

46.5[50.5:54.5]cm

sleeves

10cm

30[33.5:37.5]cm

41[42:43]cm

26cm

7cm

measures 19[19¼:19¾]in/ 48[49:50]cm from beg, ending with a Ws row and same patt row as back and front to beg of armhole shaping.

Shape top

Keeping patt correct, cast off 4 sts at beg of next 2 rows.
Dec one st at each end of next and every foll alt row until 42[52:62] sts rem.
Cast off 8[10:12] sts at beg of next 4 rows, then cast off rem 10[12:14] sts fairly loosely.

Neckband

Join right shoulder seam, carefully matching patt.
With No 10/3¼mm needles and Rs of work facing, pick up and K 72[74:76] sts evenly around front neck and 36[38:40] sts evenly across back neck. 108[112:116] sts.
Work 6 rows K1, P1 rib.
Next row (Ws) K to end to form fold-line.
Work 6 more rows K1, P1 rib as set.
Cast off loosely in rib.

To make up

Press as directed on ball band.
Join left shoulder and neckband seam.
Fold neckband in half to Ws and sl st down. Join side and sleeve seams. With centre of top of sleeve to shoulder seam, sew in sleeves.

Helping hand

Beginners and more experienced knitters will be interested in this method of casting on, which gives an edge similar to that of a machine-knitted garment. It can only be used when casting on for single, knit one, purl one rib.

Make a slip loop and cast on the next stitch.
*Insert the point of the right hand needle between the last two stitches on the left hand needle, from the *back to the front*, take the yarn over and round the needle as if to purl a stitch and draw the yarn through with the right hand needle. Put this cast on stitch on to the left hand needle.

Insert the point of the right hand needle between the last two stitches on the left hand needle, from the *front to the back*, take the yarn under and round the needle as if to knit a stitch and draw the yarn through with the right hand needle. Put this cast on stitch on to the left hand needle.

Continue from the * until the required number of stitches have been cast on. Now continue in single rib, working into the back loop of each cast on knit stitch on the first row only, and noting that an even number of stitches will begin with a knit stitch and an odd number with a purl stitch.

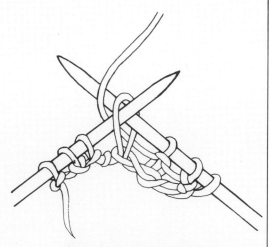

fig 1 casting on for single rib

Cable and rib jersey

This design features broken rib pattern and an unusual cable twist on the centre front, back and sleeves.

The sizes are suitable for a man or a woman and the yarn is an authentic Icelandic quality.

Measurements

To fit 34–36[38–40]in/86–91[97–102]cm bust/chest
Actual measurements 42½[46½]in/108[118]cm
Length to centre back neck, excluding neckband, 26¾[27½]in/68[70]cm
Sleeve seam, 17¼[18]in/44[46]cm
The figures in [] refer to the 38–40in/97–102cm size only

Materials

18[19] × 50g balls of Scotnord Scotia
One pair No 8/4mm needles
One pair No 6/5mm needles
Cable needle
The quantities of yarn given are based on average requirements and are approximate

Tension

17 sts and 24 rows to 4in/10cm over rib patt worked on No 6/5mm needles

Cable panel

Worked over 31 sts.
1st row (Rs) P2, K5, P1, K6, P3, K6, P1, K5, P2.
2nd row K2, P5, K1, P6, K3, P6, K1, P5, K2.
3rd row P2, K5, P1, sl next 3 sts on to cable needle and hold at back of work, K3 from left hand needle then K3 from cable needle — abbreviated as C6B —, P3, sl next 3 sts on to cable needle and hold at front of work, K3 from left hand needle then K3 from cable needle — abbreviated as C6F —, P1, K5, P2.
4th row As 2nd row.
5th to 8th rows As 1st to 4th rows.
9th row As 1st row.
10th row As 2nd row.
11th row P2, sl next 6 sts on to cable needle and hold at front of work, K6 from left hand needle then K6 from cable needle — abbreviated as C12F —, P3, sl next 6 sts on to cable needle and hold at back of work, K6 from left hand needle then K6 from cable needle — abbreviated as C12B —, P2.
12th row K2, P6, K1, P5, K3, P5, K1, P6, K2.
13th row P2, K6, P1, K5, P3, K5, P1, K6, P2.
14th row As 12th row.
15th row P2, C6F, P1, K5, P3, K5, P1, C6B, P2.
16th row As 12th row.
17th to 28th rows Rep 13th to 16th rows 3 times more.
29th row As 13th row.
30th row As 14th row.
31st row P2, C12B, P3, C12F, P2.
32nd row As 2nd row.
33rd to 40th rows Rep 1st to 4th rows twice more.
These 40 rows form the pattern.

Back

With No 8/4mm needles cast on 83[91] sts.
1st row (Rs) K1, *P1, K1, rep from * to end.
2nd row P1, *K1, P1, rep from * to end.
Rep these 2 rows until back

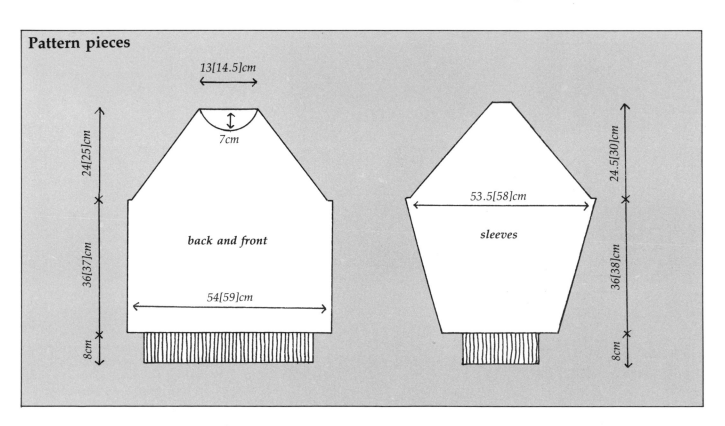

Pattern pieces

13[14.5]cm

7cm

24[25]cm

36[37]cm

8cm

back and front

54[59]cm

53.5[58]cm

sleeves

24.5[30]cm

36[38]cm

8cm

measures 3¼in/8cm from beg, ending with a 1st row.
Next row (inc row) Rib 3[7], *M1 by picking up loop lying between needles and K tbl, rib 4, rep from * to last 0[4] sts, rib 0[4] sts. 103[111] sts.
Change to No 6/5mm needles. Commence patt.
1st row (Rs) K36[40] sts, work across next 31 sts as 1st row of cable panel, K36[40] sts.
2nd row (K1, P1) 18[20] times, work across next 31 sts as 2nd row of cable panel, (P1, K1) 18[20] times.
These 2 rows set the patt. Cont in patt working cable panel on centre 31 sts, until back measures 17¼[17¾]in/44[45]cm from beg, ending with a Ws row.

Shape raglans

Keeping patt correct throughout, cast off 2[3] sts at beg of next 2 rows, then dec as foll:
1st row K2, sl 1, K1, psso, patt to last 4 sts, K2 tog, K2.
2nd row P2, P2 tog tbl, patt to last 4 sts, P2 tog, P2.
3rd row Patt to end.
4th row As 2nd row of shaping.
5th row As 1st row of shaping.
6th row Patt to end.
Rep these 6 rows until 23[25] sts rem, ending with a Ws row.
Leave sts on holder for centre back neck.

Front

Work as given for back until 43[45] sts rem in raglan shaping, ending with a Ws row.

Shape neck

Keeping raglan shaping correct, patt across 15 sts, turn, leave rem sts on a spare needle.
Complete left side first.
Dec one st at neck edge on next and foll 4 alt rows.
Cont raglan shaping until all sts are worked off.
With Rs of work facing, sl first 13[15] sts from spare needle on to holder and leave for centre front neck, rejoin yarn to rem sts and patt to end.
Complete right side to match left side reversing all shapings.

Sleeves

With No 8/4mm needles cast on 39[47] sts. Work in rib as given for back welt until sleeve measures 3¼in/8cm from beg, ending with a 1st row.
Next row (inc row) Rib 1[5], *M1 as given for back, rib 2, rep from * to last 2[6] sts, M1, rib 1[2], M1, rib 1[4] sts. 59[67] sts.
Change to No 6/5mm needles. Commence patt.
1st row (Rs) K14[18] sts, work across next 31 sts as 1st row of cable panel, K14[18] sts.

2nd row (K1, P1) 7[9] times, work across next 31 sts as 2nd row of cable panel, (P1, K1) 7[9] times.
These 2 rows set the patt.
Cont in patt working cable panel on centre 31 sts, *at the same time* inc one st at each end of 5th and every foll 4th row, working extra sts into rib at sides, until there are 91[99] sts.
Cont without shaping until sleeve measures 17¼[18]in/44[46]cm from beg, ending with a Ws row.

Shape raglan

Cast off 2[3] sts at beg of next 2 rows, then dec as foll:
1st row K2, sl 1, K1, psso, patt to last 4 sts, K2 tog, K2.
2nd row P2, P2 tog tbl, patt to last 4 sts, P2 tog, P2.
3rd row Patt to end.
4th row As 2nd shaping row.
5th row As 1st shaping row.
6th row Patt to end.
Rep these 6 rows until 11[13] sts rem, ending with a Ws row.
Leave sts on holder.

Neckband

Join raglan seams, leaving left back raglan open.
With Rs of work facing and No 8/4mm needles, K across 11[13] sts of left sleeve top, pick up and K14 sts down left front neck, K across 13[15] sts on front neck holder, pick up and K14 sts up right front neck, K across 11[13] sts of right sleeve top and 23[25] sts from back neck holder. 86[94] sts.
Work in K1, P1 rib for 2¼in/6cm. Cast off in rib.

To make up

Do not press.
Join left back raglan and neckband seam. Fold neckband in half to Ws and sl st down.
Join side and sleeve seams.

Opposite: Centre panels of thickly twisted cables on the body and sleeves highlight this jersey. The round neckline and raglan sleeves give freedom of movement, making this the ideal choice as a sports sweater. Designed by Debbie Scott.

Cable and broken rib jersey

A simple shape and super yarn have been used for this dropped shoulder line jersey, in a wide size range.

The bold centre cable panel is defined with single twist cables on either side and the rest of the jersey is worked in broken rib, with single rib edges.

Measurements

To fit 36[38:40:42:44:46:48]in/ 91[97:102:107:112:117:122]cm bust/ chest

Actual measurements, 42½[45:46½:48½:51:53:54½]in/ 108[114:118:123:129:134:138]cm

Length to shoulders, 26[26:27:27:27½:27½:27½:]in/ 66[66:68:68:70:70:70]cm

Sleeve seam, 18½[18½:19:19½:19½:19½:19¾]in/ 47[47:48:49:49:49:50]cm

The figures in [] refer to the 38/97, 40/102, 42/107, 44/112, 46/117 and 48in/122cm sizes respectively

Materials

14[15:15:16:16:17:17] × 50g balls of Jaeger Matchmaker 2 Double Knitting

One pair No 10/3¼mm needles
One pair No 8/4mm needles
Cable needle

The quantities of yarn given are based on average requirements and are approximate

Opposite: This interesting jersey features panels of wide and narrow cables, set against a broken rib pattern. The wide size range makes it suitable for a man or woman.
Designed by Debbie Jenkins.

Tension

22 sts and 30 rows to 4in/10cm over st st worked on No 8/4mm needles

Back

With No 10/3¼mm needles cast on 105[109:113:117:125:129:135] sts.

1st row (Rs) K1, *P1, K1, rep from * to end.

2nd row P1, *K1, P1, rep from * to end.

Rep these 2 rows until back measures 2¾in/7cm from beg, ending with a 2nd row.

Next row (inc row) (Rib 2, M1 by picking up loop lying between needles and K tbl) 7[11:12:13:9:10:7] times, (rib 3, M1) 25[21:21:21:29:29:35] times, (rib 2, M1) 7[11:12:13:9:10:7] times, rib 2. 144[152:158:164:172:178:184] sts.

Change to No 8/4mm needles.

Next row K44[48:51:54:58:61:64], P8, K14, P12, K14, P8, K to end.

Cont in patt as foll:

1st row (Rs) K1[1:0:1:1:0:1] st, (P1, K1) 21[23:25:26:28:30:31] times, P1, K8, (P1, K1) 6 times, P2, K12, P2, (K1, P1) 6 times, K8, P1, (K1, P1) 21[23:25:26:28:30:31] times, K1[1:0:1:1:0:1] st.

2nd and every foll alt row K44[48:51:54:58:61:64], P8, K14, P12, K14, P8, K to end.

3rd row As 1st row.

5th row K1[1:0:1:1:0:1] st, (P1, K1) 21[23:25:26:28:30:31] times, P1, sl next 4 sts on to cable needle and hold at back of work, K4 from left hand needle then K4 from cable needle — abbreviated as C8B —, (P1, K1) 6 times, P2, sl next 3 sts on to cable needle and hold at back of work, K3 from left hand needle then K3 from cable needle — abbreviated as C6B —, sl next 3 sts on to cable needle and hold at front of work, K3 from left hand needle then K3 from cable needle — abbreviated as C6F —, P2, (K1, P1) 6 times, sl next 4 sts on to cable needle and hold at front of work, K4 from left hand needle then K4 from cable needle — abbreviated as C8F —, P1, (K1, P1) 21[23:25:26:28:30:31] times, K1[1:0:1:1:0:1] st.

7th row As 1st row.

9th row K1[1:0:1:1:0:1] st, (P1, K1) 21[23:25:26:28:30:31] times, P1, K8, (P1, K1) 6 times, P2, K12, P2, (K1, P1) 6 times, K8, P1, (K1, P1) 21[23:25:26:28:30:31] times, K1[1:0:1:1:0:1]st.

10th row As 2nd row.

These 10 rows form the patt.

Cont in patt until back measures 26[26:27:27:27½:27½:27½]in/ 66[66:68:68:70:70:70]cm from beg, ending with a Ws row.

Shape shoulders

Cast off 22[24:25:26:28:29:30] sts at beg of next 2 rows, then 22[24:25:27:28:30:31] sts at beg of foll 2 rows.

Leave rem 56[56:58:58:60:60:62] sts on a spare needle for centre back neck.

Front

Work as given for back until front measures 22[22:24:24:28:28:28] rows less than back to beg of shoulder shaping, ending with a Ws row.

Shape neck

Keep patt correct throughout.

Next row Patt 52[56:58:61:64:67:69] sts, work 2 tog, turn and leave rem sts on a spare needle.

Complete left shoulder first.

Dec one st at neck edge on next 6 rows, then on foll 3 alt rows. 44[48:50:53:56:59:61] sts.

Work 9[9:11:11:15:15:15] rows without shaping, ending with a Ws row.

Shape shoulder

Cast off 22[24:25:26:28:29:30] sts at beg of next row. Work one row.

Cast off rem 22[24:25:27:28:30:31] sts.

With Rs of work facing, sl first 36[36:38:38:40:40:42] sts from spare needle on to a holder and leave for centre front neck, rejoin yarn to rem sts, work 2 tog, patt to end.

Complete right shoulder to match left, reversing all shapings and noting that an extra row will have to be worked before beg shoulder shaping.

Pattern pieces

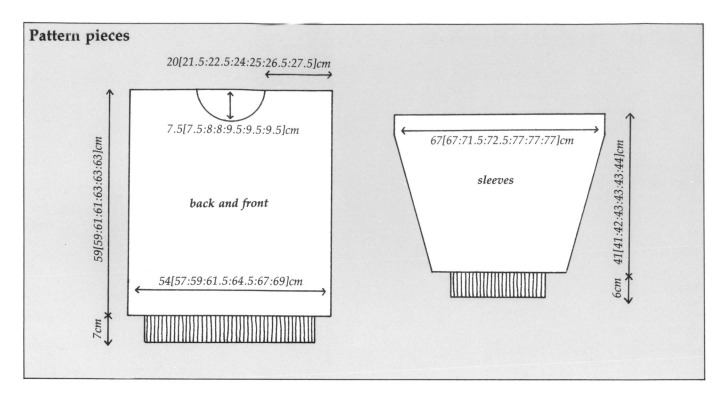

20[21.5:22.5:24:25:26.5:27.5]cm

7.5[7.5:8:8:9.5:9.5:9.5]cm

59[59:61:61:63:63:63]cm

back and front

54[57:59:61.5:64.5:67:69]cm

7cm

67[67:71.5:72.5:77:77:77]cm

sleeves

41[41:42:43:43:43:44]cm

6cm

Sleeves

With No 10/3¼mm needles cast on 51[53:55:55:57:57:59] sts.
Work 2¼in/6cm rib as given for back, ending with a 2nd row.
Next row (inc row) (Rib 2, M1 as given for back) 7[6:8:8:7:7:6] times, (rib 3, M1) 7[9:7:7:9:9:11] times, (rib 2, M1) 7[6:8:8:7:7:6] times, rib 2. 72[74:78:78:80:80:82] sts.
Change to No 8/4mm needles.
Next row K30[31:33:33:34:34:35], P12, K to end.
Cont in patt, placing first 6 rows as foll:
1st row (Rs) K0[1:1:1:0:0:1] st, (P1, K1) 14[14:15:15:16:16:16] times, P2, K12, P2, (K1, P1) 14[14:15:15:16:16:16] times, K0[1:1:1:0:0:1] st.
2nd row K30[31:33:33:34:34:35] sts, P12, K to end.
3rd row As 1st row.
4th row Inc in first st, K29[30:32:32:33:33:34] sts, P12, K to last 2 sts, inc in next st, K1.
5th row K1[0:0:0:1:1:0] st, (P1, K1) 14[15:16:16:16:16:17] times, P2, C6B, C6F, P2, (K1, P1)

14[15:16:16:16:16:17] times, K1[0:0:0:1:1:0] st.
6th row K31[32:34:34:35:35:36] sts, P12, K to end.
These 6 rows set patt.
Cont in patt as given for back as now set, inc one st at each end of next and every foll 3rd row until there are 148[148:158:160:140:140:154] sts, taking extra sts into patt.

5th, 6th and 7th sizes

Inc one st at each end of every following alt row until there are 170 sts.

All sizes

Work 7[10:5:4:7:7:7] rows without shaping, ending with a Ws row.
Cast off loosely.

Neckband

Join right shoulder seam.
With Rs of work facing and No 10/3¼mm needles, pick up and K19[19:22:22:24:24:24] sts down left side of front neck, K across

front neck sts on holder, pick up and K19[19:22:22:24:24:24] sts up right front neck, then K across back neck sts on holder dec one st in centre.
129[129:139:139:147:147:151] sts.
Beg with a 2nd row, work 2¼in/6cm rib as given for back welt, ending with a 2nd row.
Cast off loosely in rib.

To make up

Do not press.
Join left shoulder and neckband seam. Fold neckband in half to Ws and sl st down.
Place markers 11[11:11¾:11¾:12½:12½:12½]in/ 28[28:30:30:32:32:32]cm down from shoulder seams on back and front. Fold sleeves in half lengthways and place centre of cast off edge to shoulder seams and sew in place to back and front between markers.
Join side and sleeve seams.

Cable jersey with raglan sleeves

This design features rib, cable and travelling patterns to great effect. It is suitable for a man or a woman and the crew neckband can be extended to form a polo collar if required.

Measurements

To fit 34 – 36[38 – 40:42 – 44]in/86 – 91[97 – 102:107 – 112]cm bust/chest
Actual measurements, 42[46:50]in/ 107[117:127]cm
Length to centre back neck, 26[26¾:27½]in/66[68:70]cm, adjustable
Sleeve seam, 17½[18:18½]in/ 45[46:47]cm, adjustable
The figures in [] refer to the 38 – 40/97 – 102 and 42 – 44in/107 – 112cm sizes respectively

Materials

Crew neck version, 12[12:13] × 50g balls of Hayfield Hedgerow Chunky
Polo neck version, 12[13:13] balls of same
One pair No 5/5½mm needles
One pair No 3/6½mm needles
Set of four No 5/5½mm needles pointed at both ends
Cable needle
The quantities of yarn given are based on average requirements and are approximate

Tension

14 sts and 20 rows to 4in/10cm over rib patt worked on No 3/ 6½mm needles

Back

With No 5/5½mm needles cast on 71[79:87] sts.
1st row (Rs) K1, *P1, K1, rep from * to end.
2nd row P1, *K1, P1, rep from * to end.
Rep these 2 rows until work measures 2¼in/6cm from beg, ending with a 2nd row.
Next row (inc row) Rib 5[4:8], *M1 by picking up loop lying between needles and K tbl, rib 6[7:7], rep from * 9 times more, M1, rib 6[5:9]. 82[90:98] sts.
Change to No 3/6½mm needles. Commence patt.
1st row (Ws) (K1, P1, K2) 4[5:6] times, K1, P1, K6, P1, K5, P1, K2, P16, K2, (P1, K5) twice, (K1, P1, K2) 4[5:6] times, K1, P1, K1.
2nd row (K3, P1) 4[5:6] times, K3, (P4, K into front of 2nd st on left hand needle then P into first st dropping both sts off needle tog —

abbreviated as T2R —) twice, P2, K4, sl next 2 sts on to cable needle and hold at back of work, K2 from left hand needle then K2 from cable needle — abbreviated as C4B —, sl next 2 sts on to cable needle and hold at front of work, K2 from left hand needle then K2 from cable needle — abbreviated as C4F —, K4, P2, (P into back of 2nd st on left hand needle then K first st dropping both sts off needle tog — abbreviated as T2L —, P4) twice, (K3, P1) 4[5:6] times, K3.
3rd row (K1, P1, K2) 4[5:6] times, K1, P1, (K5, P1) twice, K3, P16, K3, P1, K5, P1, K4, (K1, P1, K2) 4[5:6] times, K1, P1, K1.
4th row (K3, P1) 4[5:6] times, K3, P3, T2R, P4, T2R, P3, K2, C4B, K4, C4F, K2, P3, T2L, P4, T2L, P3, (K3, P1) 4[5:6] times, K3.
5th row (K1, P1, K2) 4[5:6] times, K1, P1, K4, P1, K5, P1, K4, P16, K4, P1, K5, P1, K3, (K1, P1, K2) 4[5:6] times, K1, P1, K1.
6th row (K3, P1) 4[5:6] times, K3, P2, (T2R, P4) twice, C4B, K8, C4F, (P4, T2L) twice, P2, (K3, P1) 4[5:6] times, K3.
7th row (K1, P1, K2) 4[5:6] times, K1, P1, K3, (P1, K5) twice, P16, (K5, P1) twice, K2, (K1, P1, K2) 4[5:6] times, K1, P1, K1.
8th row (K3, P1) 4[5:6] times, K3, P2, (T2L, P4) twice, K4, C4B, C4F,

Pattern pieces

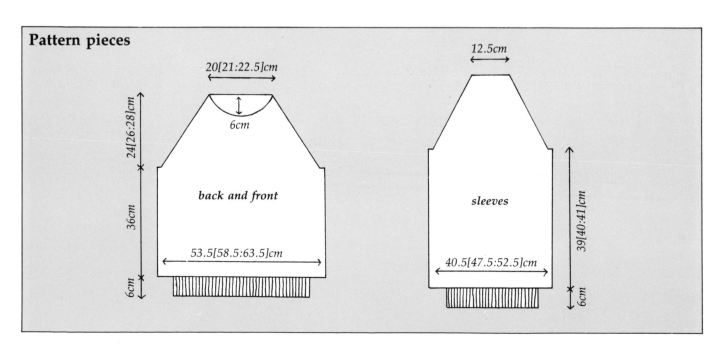

20[21:22.5]cm
6cm
24[26:28]cm
36cm
6cm
back and front
53.5[58.5:63.5]cm

12.5cm
39[40:41]cm
6cm
sleeves
40.5[47.5:52.5]cm

K4, (P4, T2R) twice, P2, (K3, P1) 4[5:6] times, K3.
9th row As 5th row.
10th row (K3, P1) 4[5:6] times, K3, P3, T2L, P4, T2L, P3, K2, C4B, K4, C4F, K2, P3, T2R, P4, T2R, P3, (K3, P1) 4[5:6] times, K3.
11th row As 3rd row.
12th row (K3, P1) 4[5:6] times, K3, (P4, T2L) twice, P2, C4B, K8, C4F, P2, (T2R, P4) twice, (K3, P1) 4[5:6] times, K3.
These 12 rows form the patt. Cont in patt until back measures 16½/ 42cm from beg or required length to underarm, ending with a Ws row.

Shape raglans
Keeping patt correct throughout, cast off 4[5:6] sts at beg of next 2 rows.
Next row K2, K2 tog, patt to last 4 sts, sl 1, K1, psso, K2.
Next row P2, patt to last 2 sts, P2.
Rep last 2 rows until 28[30:32] sts rem. Work one row without shaping.
Leave rem sts on holder for back neck.

Front
Work as given for back, shaping raglans until 36[38:40] sts rem. Work one row without shaping.

Shape neck
Next row K2, K2 tog, patt 5 sts, turn and leave rem sts on a spare needle.
Next row P2 tog tbl, patt 4 sts, P2.
Next row K2, K2 tog, patt 3 sts.
Next row P2 tog tbl, patt 2 sts, P2.
Next row K2, K2 tog, K1.
Next row P2 tog tbl, P2.
Next row K1, K2 tog.
Next row P2.
Cast off.

With right side of work facing, sl first 18[20:22] sts from spare needle on to holder for centre front neck, rejoin yarn to neck edge of rem sts, patt to last 4 sts, sl 1, K1, psso, K2.
Complete to match first side, reversing all shapings.

Sleeves
With No 5/5½mm needles cast on 33[35:37] sts. Work 2¼in/6cm rib as given for back welt, ending with a 2nd row, and inc one st at end of row on 3rd size only.
Next row (inc row) Rib 4[2:1], *M1 as given for back, rib 1, rep from * 23[29:34] times more, M1, rib 5[3:1]. 58[66:74] sts.
Change to No 3/6½mm needles.
Cont in patt as foll:
1st row (Ws) (K1, P1, K2) 4[5:6] times, K1, P1, K3, P16, K2, (K1, P1, K2) 4[5:6] times, K1, P1, K1.
2nd row (K3, P1) 4[5:6] times, K3, P2, K4, C4B, C4F, K4, P2, (K3, P1) 4[5:6] times, K3.
3rd row As 1st row.
4th row (K3, P1) 4[5:6] times, K3, P2, K2, C4B, K4, C4F, K2, P2, (K3, P1) 4[5:6] times, K3.
5th row As 1st row.
6th row (K3, P1) 4[5:6] times, K3, P2, C4B, K8, C4F, P2, (K3, P1) 4[5:6] times, K3.
Rep these 6 rows until sleeve measures 17½[18:18½]in/ 45[46:47]cm from beg, or required length to underarm, ending with a Ws row.

Shape raglan top
Keeping patt correct throughout cast off 4[5:6] sts at beg of next 2 rows.
Next row K2, K2 tog, patt to last 4 sts, sl 1, K1, psso, K2.

Next row P2, patt to last 2 sts, P2.
Next row K2, patt to last 2 sts, K2.
Next row P2, patt to last 2 sts, P2.
Rep last 4 rows until 34[42:50] sts rem. Work one row without shaping.
Next row K2, K2 tog, patt to last 4 sts, sl 1, K1, psso, K2.
Next row P2, patt to last 2 sts, P2.
Rep last 2 rows until 18 sts rem. Work one row without shaping.
Leave sts on holder.

Neckband (optional)
Join raglan seams.
With right side of work facing and set of four No 5/5½mm needles, K across back neck sts on holder dec 7 sts evenly, K2 tog at seam then cont across left sleeve sts on holder dec 6 sts evenly, pick up and K7 sts down left front neck, K across front neck sts on holder dec 5 sts evenly, pick up and K7 sts up right front neck, K across right sleeve sts on holder dec 6 sts evenly and K last st of sleeve tog with first st of back neck. 70[74:78] sts. **.
Work 2¾in/7cm in rounds of K1, P1 rib.
Cast off loosely in rib.

Polo collar (optional)
Work as given for neckband to **.
Work 7¾in/20cm in rounds of K1, P1 rib.
Cast off loosely in rib.

To make up
Do not press.
Join side and sleeve seams.
Either fold neckband in half to Ws and sl st down, or fold polo collar in half to outside.

Opposite: Cables, ribs and travelling stitches are all used in this highly-textured jersey, suitable for a man or woman. It can be completed with a crew neckband or a polo collar.
Designed by Sue Roberts.

Plaited cable and twisted rib jersey

This design has a central panel of plaited cables on the back and front. The sleeves also feature this central panel, which continues as a saddle top shoulder.
The jersey is suitable for a man or woman and has a neat, double crew neckline.

Measurements

To fit 38[40:42]in/97[102:107]cm bust/chest
Actual measurements, 43[46:49]in/110[117:124]cm
Length to shoulders, approximately 24¾[25¼:26¼]in/63[64:66]cm
Sleeve seam, 17½[17¾:18]in/44[45:47]cm
The figures in [] refer to the 40/102 and 42in/107cm sizes respectively

Materials

13[14:15] × 50g balls of Emu Superwash wool Double Knitting
One pair No 10/3¼mm needles
One pair No 8/4¼mm needles
Cable needle
The quantities of yarn given are based on average requirements and are approximate

Tension

Central cable panel of 24 sts 3in/7.5cm in width; 2 twisted st panels of 16 sts 2½in/6.5cm in width; 30 rows of twisted st panels 4in/10cm in length worked on No 8/4mm needles

Cable panel pattern

Worked as a central panel of 24 sts on body and sleeves.
1st row (Rs) P2, K3, P4, sl next 3 sts on to cable needle and hold at back of work, K3 from left hand needle then K3 from cable needle—abbreviated as C6B–, P4, K3, P2.
2nd and every foll alt row K all K sts and P all P sts as they appear, noting that this row will read K2, P3, K4, P6, K4, P3, K2.

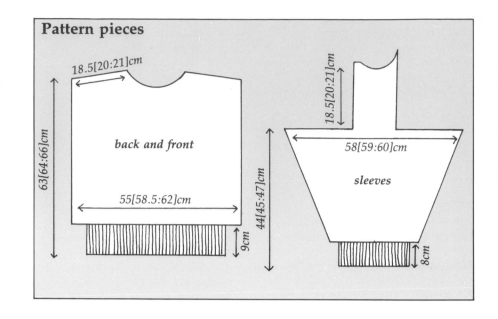

Pattern pieces

18.5[20:21]cm

back and front

63[64:66]cm

55[58.5:62]cm

9cm

18.5[20:21]cm

58[59:60]cm

sleeves

44[45:47]cm

8cm

3rd row P2, (sl next 3 sts on to cable needle and hold at front of work, P1 from left hand needle then K3 from cable needle–abbreviated as C4F–, P2, sl next st on to cable needle and hold at back of work, K3 from left hand needle then P1 from cable needle–abbreviated as C4B) twice, P2.
5th row P3, C4F, C4B, P2, C4F, C4B, P3.
7th row P4, sl next 3 sts on to cable needle and hold at front of work, K3 from left hand needle then K3 from cable needle–abbreviated as C6F–, P4, C6B, P4.
9th row P3, C4B, C4F, P2, C4B, C4F, P3.
11th row P2, (C4B, P2, C4F) twice, P2.
13th row P2, K3, P4, C6F, P4, K3, P2.
15th row As 3rd row.
17th row As 5th row.
19th row P4, C6B, P4, C6F, P4.
21st row As 9th row.
23rd row As 11th row.
24th row As 2nd row.
These 24 rows form patt.

Back

With No 10/3¼mm needles cast on 117[125:133] sts.
1st row (Rs) P1, *K1, P1, rep from * to end.

2nd row K1, *P1, K1, rep from * to end.
Rep these 2 rows for 3½in/9cm, ending with a 1st row.
Next row (inc row) Rib 2[6:2], (M1 by picking up loop lying between needles and K tbl, rib 11, M1, rib 3) 3 times, M1, rib 9[9:17], (M1, rib 3) 3 times, M1 rib 19, (M1, rib 3, M1, rib 11) twice, M1, rib 3, M1, rib 5[9:13]. 134[142:150] sts.
Change to No 8/4mm needles.
Commence cable and twisted rib patt.
1st base row P3[7:3], (K into back of 2nd st on left hand needle then K into first st slipping both sts off needle tog–abbreviated as T2K–, P6) 6[6:7] times, T2K, P4, K20, P4, (T2K, P6) 6[6:7] times, T2K, P3[7:3].

*Opposite: The distinctive saddle-top shoulder line is the focal point of this jersey.
Designed by Jan Bird.*

2nd base row K3[7:3], (P into front of 2nd st on the left hand needle then P into first st slipping both sts off needle tog–abbreviated as T2P–, K6) 6[6:7] times, T2P, K4, P20, K4, (T2P, K6) 6[6:7] times, T2P, K3[7:3].
1st patt row (Rs) P3[7:3], (T2K, P6) 6[6:7] times, T2K, P2, work 1st row of cable panel patt across next 24 sts, P2, (T2K, P6) 6[6:7] times, T2K, P3[7:3].
2nd patt row K3[7:3], (T2P, K6) 6[6:7] times, T2P, K2, work 2nd row of cable panel patt across next 24 sts, K2 (T2P, K6) 6[6:7] times, T2P, K3[7:3].
These 2 rows establish position of central cable panel, with twisted ribs on either side.
Cont in patt, working appropriate rows of cable panel patt, until work measures 22½[22¾:23¾]in/57[58:59]cm from beg, ending with a 4th[6th:8th] row of cable panel patt.

Shape neck

Next row Patt 54[57:60] sts, turn and leave rem sts on a spare needle.
Complete this side first.
Cast off 3 sts at beg of next and foll 2 alt rows. 45[48:51]sts.
Work 2 rows in patt. Cast off in patt.
With Rs of work facing, sl first 26[28:30] sts from spare needle on to holder and leave for centre neck, rejoin yarn to next st and patt 54[57:60] sts to end.
Work one row. Work as given for first side from ** to **. Work one row.
Cast off in patt.

Front

Work as given for back.

Left sleeve

***With No 10/3¼mm needles cast on 53[53:57] sts.
1st row (Rs) K1, *P1, K1, rep from * to end.
2nd row P1, *K1, P1, rep from * to end.
Rep these 2 rows for 3½in/8cm, ending with a first row.
Next row (inc row) Rib 4[2:6], *M1,

rib 1, M1, rib 2, rep from * 14[15:14] times more, M1, rib 4[3:6]. 84[86:88] sts.
Change to No 8/4mm needles.
Commence patt.
1st base row P2[3:4], (T2K, P6) 3 times, T2K, P4, K20, P4, (T2K, P6) 3 times, T2K, P2[3:4].
2nd base row K2[3:4], (T2P, K6) 3 times, T2P, K4, P20, K4 (T2P, K6) 3 times, T2P, K2[3:4].
1st patt row (Rs) P2[3:4], (T2K, P6) 3 times, T2K, P2, work 1st row of cable panel patt across next 24 sts, P2, (T2K, P6) 3 times, T2K, P2[3:4].
2nd patt row K2[3:4], (T2P, K6) 3 times, T2P, K2, work 2nd row of cable panel patt across next 24 sts, K2, (T2P, K6) 3 times, T2P, K2[3:4].
These 2 rows establish position of central cable panel, with twisted ribs on either side.
Cont in patt as now set, inc one st at each end of next and every foll 4th row and working extra sts into twisted rib patt, until there are 146[148:150] sts.
Cont in patt without shaping until sleeve measures 17½[17¾:18]in/44[45:47]cm from beg, ending with a Ws row.

Shape saddle shoulder

Cast off 54[55:56] sts at beg of next 2 rows. 38 sts.
Cont in patt on rem sts until saddle shoulder extension fits along cast off edge of back or front, ending with a Ws row.***

Shape for neck

Next row Patt 19 sts, turn and leave rem sts on a spare needle.
Cast off 3 sts at beg of next and foll 2 alt rows, then 2 sts at beg of foll 2 alt rows.
Dec one st at neck edge on every row until 2 sts rem. Work 2 sts tog and fasten off.
With Rs of work facing, rejoin yarn to first st on spare needle, cast off 7 sts, patt to end of row. 12 sts.
Patt one row. Cast off 4 sts at beg of next and foll alt row. Cast off rem 4 sts.

Right sleeve

Work as given for left sleeve from *** to ***.

Shape for neck

Next row Patt 12sts, turn and leave rem sts on a spare needle.
Cast off 4 sts at beg of next and foll alt row. Patt one row. Cast off rem 4 sts.
With Rs of work facing, rejoin yarn to first st on spare needle, cast off 7 sts, patt to end of row. 19 sts. Patt one row.
Cast off 3 sts at beg of next and foll 2 alt rows. Dec one st at neck edge on every row until 2 sts rem. Work 2 sts tog and fasten off.

Neckband

Join cast off edges of back and front to row ends of saddle shoulder extensions, leaving left back seam open.
Place a coloured marker on back cast off edge.
With Rs of work facing and No 10/3¼mm needles, rejoin yarn to left sleeve top, pick up and K30 sts evenly round sleeve top, 12 sts down left front neck, work across neck sts on holder as foll:-
K2[3:4], (K2 tog, K2) twice, (K2 tog) 3 times, (K2, K2 tog) twice, K2[3:4], pick up and K12 sts up right front neck, 30 sts evenly round sleeve top, 12 sts down right back neck, rep from ** to ** once across neck sts on holder, pick up and K12 sts up left back neck. 146[150:154] sts.
Next row (dec row) P12[10:8], *P2 tog, P2, rep from * to last 14[12:10] sts, P2 tog, P12[10:8] sts. 115[117:119] sts.
Work 3½in/9cm rib as given for back welt. Cast off in rib.

To make up

Press lightly as directed on ball band.
Join left back shoulder and neckband seam. Fold neckband in half to Ws and sl st down.
Fold sleeves in half lengthways and sew in place.
Join side and sleeve seams.

Channel Islands knitting

*Harry Freeman, sole survivor of the Whitby lifeboat disaster in 1881,
is seen here wearing his authentic guernsey, which would have helped him
withstand gruelling weather and working conditions.*

Channel Islands knitting

Trying to research the history of regional knitting is most frustrating, as there are huge gaps in reference sources and many documented reports contradict each other. It cannot be said with any degree of certainty whether fishermens' knitting developed from the type of knitting produced in the Channel Isles, or vice versa. What can be deduced is that the garments originated in the sister islands of Guernsey and Jersey which eventually gave their names to two completely different concepts in knitting, were almost identical in shape to fishermens' ganseys. The main difference between the garments from the two islands appears to be that the original guernseys were invariably knitted in plain stocking stitch in heavy yarn, while jerseys were worked in finer yarn in a variety of colours.

In the early days, Jersey appears to have had the more flourishing trade in knitting, becoming involved in a Newfoundland enterprise in the seventeenth century which resulted in an exchange of shipbuilding expertise with woollen garments for some considerable time. One particular item which formed part of this regular trade was a long, fisherman's stocking cap, complete with a pompon on the end. Accounts differ as to whether these were knitted in red wool or in a natural colour, but a mid-nineteenth century painting in the Société Jersiaise Museum depicts fishermen who appear to be wearing red caps.

Towards the end of the nineteenth century, the fleece from the sheep grazed in Jersey was taken to Normandy to be spun into wool. This journey was undertaken by the shepherds' wives, who set off from various locations in the island, but mainly from St. Ouens. The wool was reputedly returned undyed and still containing its natural lanolin, so it would have been grey in colour, rather than cream or natural. From this report it would appear that any subsequent scouring and dyeing processes must have been undertaken on the island, using local or imported dye sources. Knitting obviously still continues to flourish in Jersey, but the name today has become synonymous with a particular style of garment, rather than a specific technique.

On the sister island of Guernsey, early examples of traditional garments were almost always unpatterned, except for a narrow band of patterning around the edge of the armholes. The shape of these garments was very square and similar to the short smock worn by farm workers in the past. The quality of the wool and the expertise which went into knitting and designing these garments, resulted in hard-wearing 'guernseys', able to withstand harsh working and weather conditions. The methods of knitting gradually progressed to include such features as gussets at the neck edge and underarms, a garter stitch welt, slits at the sides for ease of movement and set in sleeves, with the armholes cut, then turned under and hemmed or with provision made for an armhole opening as the body was knitted. Double ribbing of knit two, purl two was used for the cuffs and wide neckband.

Today we tend to think of authentic guernseys as having flat, brocade-like patterning on the yoke, or as an all-over fabric. They are still knitted in the round but on a circular needle rather than sets of as many as eight needles to take all the stitches. Some modern designs are knitted in sections, with the front and back body and sleeves all knitted separately and sewn together. The texture and colour of the wool used to knit guernseys does much to help them retain their distinctive appearance. Special five ply wool is still available in the traditional navy blue, but cream and red can also be obtained.

This section of the book continues with row-by-row instructions for some of the stitch patterns used in designing guernseys. The garments which follow have been especially designed to include authentic features which will still meet today's requirements.

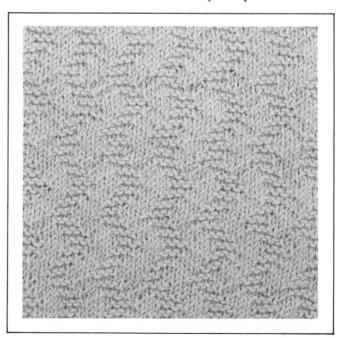

Traditional guernsey patterns

These are numerous but they all have one thing in common – a brocade-type fabric which shows knit stitches against a purl background, or purl stitches against a knit background.

Betty Martin's pattern

This simple stitch is most effective when worked as a panel between more complicated patterns. It requires multiples of 4 stitches, plus 2, eg 18.

1st row (Rs) *K2, P2, rep from * to last 2 sts, K2.
2nd row *P2, K2, rep from * to last 2 sts, P2.
3rd row K to end.
4th row P to end.
These 4 rows form the pattern.

Tree of life pattern

This is based on the shape of a fern or pine cone. It is interesting to note that the same motif has been adapted into a traditional Fair Isle two-colour pattern. This sample has been worked as a panel of 15 stitches.

1st row (Rs), K7, P1, K7.
2nd row P7, K1, P7.
3rd row As 1st row.
4th row P6, K1, P1, K1, P6.
5th row K5, P1, K3, P1, K5.
6th row P4, (K1, P2) twice, K1, P4.
7th row K3, P1, K2, P1, K1, P1, K2, P1, K3.
8th row P2, K1, P2, K1, P3, K1, P2, K1, P2.
9th row K1, P1, (K2, P1) 4 times, K1.
10th row P3, K1, P2, K1, P1, K1, P2, K1, P3.
11th row K2, P1, K2, P1, K3, P1, K2, P1, K2.
12th row As 6th row.
13th row As 7th row.
14th row P5, K1, P3, K1, P5.
15th row K4, (P1, K2) twice, P1, K4.
16th row As 4th row.
17th row As 5th row.
18th row P7, K1, P7.
19th row K6, P1, K1, P1, K6.
20th row P to end.
These 20 rows form the pattern.

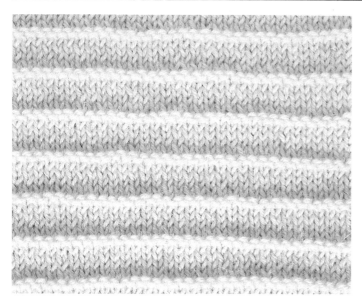

Ladder pattern

This is another very simple stitch which can be worked as a panel. It can be worked over any number of stitches.

1st row (Rs) K to end.
2bd row P to end.
Rep these 2 rows once, or twice more depending on depth of ladder required, then rep 1st row once more.
Next row K to end.
These 6 or 8 rows form the pattern.

Flag pattern

This pattern, known as 'kilt' pattern in Scotland, forms a pennant shape against the background and is a reversible pattern. This sample has been worked as a panel of 8 stitches, with 4 moss stitches on either side, eg 16 sts.

1st row (Rs) (K1, P1) twice, K1, P7, (K1, P1) twice.
2nd row (K1, P1) twice, K6, P2, (K1, P1) twice.
3rd row (P1, K1) twice, K3, P5, (P1, K1) twice.
4th row (P1, K1) twice, K4, P4, (P1, K1) twice.
5th row (K1, P1) twice, K5, P3, (K1, P1) twice.
6th row (K1, P1) twice, K2, P6, (K1, P1) twice.
7th row (P1, K1) twice, K7, P1, (P1, K1) twice.
8th row (P1, K1) twice, P8, (P1, K1) twice.
These 8 rows form the pattern.

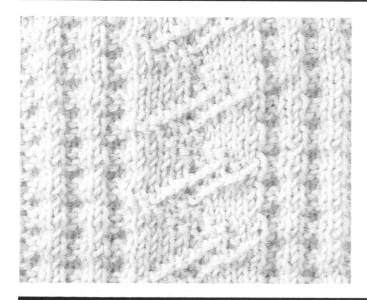

Marriage lines pattern

Zigzag patterns are used to depict paths up cliff faces, or lightning, but this double zigzag version is of Scottish origin and represents the ups and downs of married life! This sample has been worked as a panel over 11 stitches.

1st row (Rs) K5, P1, K2, P1, K2.
2nd row P1, K1, P2, K1, P6.
3rd row As 1st row.
4th row P3, K1, P2, K1, P4.
5th row K3, P1, K2, P1, K4.
6th row P5, K1, P2, K1, P2.
7th row K1, P1, K2, P1, K6.
8th row P5, K1, P2, K1, P2.
9th row K3, P1, K2, P1, K4.
10th row P3, K1, P2, K1, P4.
These 10 rows form the pattern.

Seeded diamond pattern

There are dozens of versions of diamond pattern which represent wealth and when enclosed with a travelling stitch outline, a field. This sample features a moss-stitch diamond against a stocking stitch background and is worked as a panel of 15 stitches.

1st row (Rs) K to end.
2nd row P to end.
3rd row K7, P1, K7.
4th row P7, K1, P7.
5th row K6, P1, K1, P1, K6.
6th row P6, K1, P1, K1, P6.
7th row K5, (P1, K1) twice, P1, K5.
8th row P5, (K1, P1) twice, K1, P5.
9th row K4, (P1, K1) 3 times, P1, K4.
10th row P4, (K1, P1) 3 times, K1, P4.
11th row K3, (P1, K1) 4 times, P1, K3.
12th row P3, (K1, P1) 4 times, K1, P3.
13th row K2, (P1, K1) 5 times, P1, K2.
14th row P2, (K1, P1) 5 times, K1, P2.
15th row K1, (P1, K1) 6 times, P1, K1.
16th row P1, (K1, P1) 6 times, K1, P1.
17th row As 13th row.
18th row As 14th row.
19th row As 11th row.
20th row As 12th row.
21st row As 9th row.
22nd row As 10th row.
23rd row As 7th row.
24th row As 8th row.
25th row As 5th row.
26th row As 6th row.
27th row As 3rd row.
28th row As 4th row.
29th row As 1st row.
30th row As 2nd row.
These 30 rows form the pattern.

Opposite: This simple version of a traditional 'gansey' has the minimum of shaping and is worked in an authentic yarn. It has a crew neckband and dropped shoulder-line, see pattern on page 38 Designed by Fiona McTague.

Guernsey-style sweater

This stylish design features zig-zag patterns on the body, divided by bands of garter stitch. The sleeves are worked in plain stocking stitch, finished with a band of garter stitch at the top. An authentic Guernsey 5 ply is used for the sweater, which is in a range of sizes, suitable for a man or a woman.

Measurements

To fit 34[36:38:40:42]in/ 86[91:97:102:107]cm bust/chest
Actual measurements, 41[43:45:47:49]in/ 104[109:114:119:124]cm
Length to shoulders, 27½in/70cm for all sizes
Sleeve seam, 19[19¼:19¾:20:20]in/ 48[49:50:51:51]cm
The figures in [] refer to the 36/91, 38/97, 40/102 and 42in/107cm sizes respectively

Materials

16[17:18:19:19] × 50g balls of Emu Guernsey 5 ply wool
One pair No 12/2¾mm needles
One pair No 9/3½mm needles
The quantities of yarn given are based on average requirements and are approximate

Tension

25 sts and 36 rows to 4in/10cm over zig-zag patt worked on No 9/3¾mm needles

Back

With No 12/2¾mm needles cast on 114[118:124:130:134] sts. Work 3¼in/8cm K1, P1 rib, ending with a Rs row.
Next row (inc row) Rib 5[6:2:5:10], *M1 by picking up loop lying between needles and K tbl, rib 8[7:7:7:6], rep from * 12[14:16:16:18] times more, M1, rib 5[7:3:6:10] sts. 128[134:142:148:154] sts.
Change to No 9/3¾mm needles.
Cont in patt as given in chart A, rep 12 rows until back measures 13½in/34cm from beg, ending with a 12th row.
Work 8 rows g st.
Cont in patt as foll:
1st row (Rs) *K1, P1, rep from * to end.
2nd row As 1st row.
3rd row *P1, K1, rep from * to end.
4th row As 3rd row.
Rep these 4 rows until back measures 17in/43cm from beg, ending with a 4th row.
Work 8 rows g st.
Beg with a Rs row, cont in patt

from chart B, rep 10 rows until back measures 27½in/70cm from beg, ending with a 10th row.

Shape shoulders

Cast off 39[41:44:46:49] sts at beg of next 2 rows.
Leave rem 50[52:54:56:56] sts on holder for centre back neck.

Front

Work as given for back until front measures 24¾in/63cm from beg, ending with a Ws row.

Shape neck

Keep patt correct throughout.
Next row Patt 52[54:57:60:62] sts, turn and leave rem sts on a spare needle.
Complete left shoulder first. Dec one st at neck edge on every row until 43[45:49:51:54] sts rem, then dec one st at neck edge and every foll alt row until 39[41:44:46:49] sts rem.
Cont without shaping until front measures same as back to shoulder, ending at side edge.
Cast off rem sts.
With Rs of work facing, sl first 24[26:28:28:30] sts from spare needle on to holder and leave for

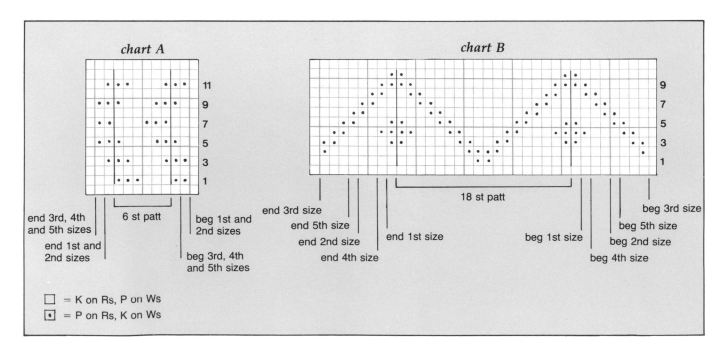

chart A

11
9
7
5
3
1

end 3rd, 4th and 5th sizes
end 1st and 2nd sizes
6 st patt
beg 1st and 2nd sizes
beg 3rd, 4th and 5th sizes

chart B

9
7
5
3
1

18 st patt

end 3rd size
end 5th size
end 2nd size
end 4th size
end 1st size
beg 1st size
beg 4th size
beg 2nd size
beg 5th size
beg 3rd size

Pattern pieces

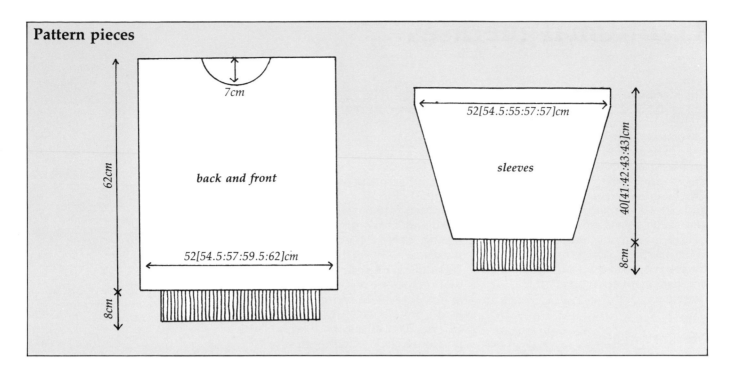

back and front

62cm

8cm

7cm

52[54.5:57:59.5:62]cm

sleeves

52[54.5:55:57:57]cm

40[41:42:43:43]cm

8cm

centre front neck, rejoin yarn to rem sts and patt to end.
Complete right shoulder to match left, reversing shapings.

Sleeves

With No 12/2¾mm needles cast on 56[60:64:64:66] sts. Work 3¼in/8cm Kl, Pl rib, ending with a Rs row.
Next row (inc row) Rib 6[4:6:6:3], *Ml as given for back welt, rib 4, rep from * 10[12:12:12:14] times more, Ml, rib 6[4:6:6:3].
68[74:78:78:82] sts.
Change to No 9/3¾mm needles.
Beg with a K row, cont in st st inc one st at each end of next and

every foll 4th row until there are 132[136:138:142:142] sts.
Cont without shaping until sleeve measures 17¾[18:18½:19:19]in/45[46:47:48:48]cm from beg, ending with a Ws row.
Change to No 12/2¾mm needles and work 1¼in/3cm g st.
Cast off loosely.

Neckband

Join right shoulder seam.
With Rs of work facing and No 12/2¾mm needles, pick up and K21[22:23:24:24] sts down left side of front neck, K across front neck sts on holder, pick up and K21[22:23:24:24] sts up right side

of front neck and K across back neck sts on holder.
116[122:128:132:134] sts.
Work 3¼in/8cm K1, P1 rib.
Cast off loosely in rib.

To make up

Press as directed on ball band, omitting ribbing.
Join left shoulder and neckband seam. Fold neckband in half to Ws and sl st down.
Fold sleeves in half lengthways, place fold to shoulder seam and sew in sleeves.
Join side and sleeve seams.

Helping hand

When knitting a garment in rows, a new ball of yarn or a new colour should always be joined in at the beginning of a row. The neatest way is to make a reef knot by passing the end of the old ball of yarn from left to right over and then under the end from the new ball. Pass the same end from right to left over and under the other end and tighten up the knot.

When knitting a guernsey in rounds, the ends of the old and new balls of yarn should always be spliced together in the course of working a round. Unravel the ends of each ball and cut away one or two strands, then overlay the two ends from opposite directions and twist them firmly together. The twisted ends should be the same thickness as the original yarn. Work a few stitches very carefully with the twisted yarn, trim away the ends.

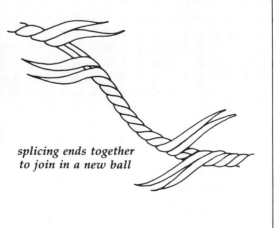

splicing ends together to join in a new ball

Traditional guernsey

This design is knitted mainly in the round and the work is divided at the underarms before commencing the front and back yoke. The sleeves are picked up round the armholes and knitted in the round down to the cuff. Provision is made for mock side and sleeves seams and underarm and neck gussets are worked for ease of movement. Simple but effective stitch patterns are used for the yoke and the welt, cuffs and neckband are worked in double rib.

Measurements

To fit 34[36:38:40]in/ 86[91:97:102]cm bust/chest
Actual measurements, 38[40:42:44]in/97[102:107:112]cm
Length to shoulders, 24½[25½:26:27]in/63[65:67:69]cm, adjustable
Sleeve seam, 18[18½:19:19½]in/ 46[47:48:49]cm, adjustable
The figures in [] refer to the 36/91, 38/97 and 40in/102cm sizes respectively

Materials

15[15:16:16] × 50g balls of Wendy Kintyre
One pair No 9/3¾mm needles
One pair No 7/4½mm needles
Set of four No 9/3¾mm needles pointed at both ends
Set of four No 7/4½mm needles pointed at both ends
One No 7/4½mm circular needle
The quantities of yarn given are based on average requirements and are approximate

Tension

19 sts and 24 rows to 4in/10cm over st st worked on No 7/4½mm needles

Body

With pair of No 9/3¾mm needles cast on 88[96:100:108] sts.
1st rib row K1, *K2, P2, rep from * to last 3 sts, K3.

2nd rib row K1, *P2, K2, rep from * to last 3 sts, P2, K1.
Rep these 2 rows 5 times more, inc one st at each end of last row for 1st and 3rd sizes only. 90[96:102:108] sts.
Break off yarn and leave these sts for time being.
Work second rib welt in same way but do not break off yarn.
Change to No 7/4½mm circular needles.
1st round With yarn attached work across second rib welt by inc in first st and K to end, then work across first rib welt in same way. 182[194:206:218] sts.
Join into a circle, making sure sts are not twisted round needle.
Place a sl loop of contrast yarn on right hand needle to denote beg of rounds.
2nd round *Pl for mock side seam, K90[96:102:108] sts, rep from * once more.
3rd round K to end.
Rep these 2 rounds until body measures 15[15¾:15¾:16½]in/ 38[40:40:42]cm from beg of ribbing, or required length to underarm less 2in/5cm, ending at sl marker.

Shape underarm gussets
1st round *Ml by picking up loop lying between needles and K tbl, K1, M1, K90[96:102:108] sts, rep from * once more. 186[198:210:222] sts.
2nd round K to end.
3rd round *M1, K3, M1, K90[96:102:108] sts, rep from * once more. 190[202:214:226] sts.
Cont inc in this way on every foll alt round until there are 206[218:230:242] sts, ending with an inc round.

Divide for armholes
1st row K13 sts and sl them on to a holder for gusset, K90[96:102:108] sts, turn and leave rem sts on a spare needle.
Complete front yoke first.

Front yoke
2nd row K1, P to last st, K1.
3rd row As 2nd row.
4th row K to end.

5th row K to end.
6th row As 2nd row.
7th row As 2nd row.

1st size
8th row K to end, inc one st in centre. 91 sts.

2nd size
8th row K to end, inc one st at each end and one st in centre. 99 sts.

3rd size
8th row K to end, dec one st at each end and one st in centre. 99 sts.

4th size
8th row K to end, dec one st in centre. 107 sts.

All sizes
Commence yoke patt as foll:
1st row (Rs) K1, *P2, K11, (P2, K2) 6[7:7:8] times, rep from * once more, P2, K11, P2, K1.
2nd row K1, *K2, P11, (K2, P2) 6[7:7:8] times, rep from * once more, K2, P11, K3.
3rd row K1, *P2, K11, P2, K22[26:26:30], rep from * once more, P2, K11, P2, K1.
4th row K1, *K2, P11, K2, P22[26:26:30], rep from * once more, K2, P11, K3.
5th row K1, *P2, K5, P1, K5, (P2, K2) 6[7:7:8] times, rep from * once more, P2, K5, P1, K5, P2, K1.
6th row K1, *K2, P4, K1, P1, K1, P4, (K2, P2) 6[7:7:8] times, rep from * once more, K2, P4, K1, P1, K1, P4, K3.
7th row K1, *P2, K3, (P1, K1) twice, P1, K3, P2, K22[26:26:30], rep from * once more, P2, K3, (P1, K1) twice, P1, K3, P2, K1.

Opposite: The body and sleeves of this authentic 'gansey' are knitted in the round and it also features traditional underarm and neckband gussets.
Designed by Betty Barnden.

Pattern pieces

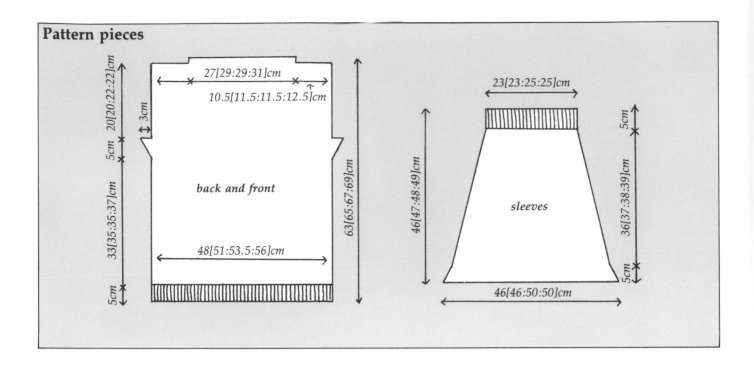

8th row K1, *K2, P2, K1, P5, K1, P2, K2, P22[26:26:30], rep from * once more, K2, P2, K1, P5, K1, P2, K3.

9th row K1, *P2, K1, (P1, K3) twice, P1, K1, (P2, K2) 6[7:7:8] times, rep from * once more, P2, K1, (P1, K3) twice, P1, K1, P2, K1.

10th row K1, *K2, P1, K1, P7, K1, P1, (K2, P2) 6[7:7:8] times, rep from * once more, K2, P1, K1, P7, K1, P1, K3.

11th row K1, *P2, K5, P1, K5, P2, K22[26:26:30], rep from * once more, P2, K5, P1, K5, P2, K1.

12th row As 4th row.

13th row As 5th row.

14th row As 2nd row.

15th row K1, *P2, K3, P5, K3, P2, K22[26:26:30], rep from * once more, P2, K3, P5, K3, P2, K1.

16th row K1, *K2, P3, K5, P3, K2, P22[26:26:30], rep from * once more, K2, P3, K5, P3, K3.

17th row K1, *P2, K3, P5, K3, (P2, K2) 6[7:7:8] times, rep from * once more, P2, K3, P5, K3, P2, K1.

18th row As 2nd row.

19th row As 11th row.

20th row As 4th row.

21st row K1, *P2, K4, P1, K1, P1, K4, (P2, K2) 6[7:7:8] times, rep from * once more, P2, K4, P1, K1, P1, K4, P2, K1.

22nd row K1, *K2, (P3, K1) twice, P3, (K2, P2) 6[7:7:8] times, rep from * once more, K2, (P3, K1) twice, P3, K3.

23rd row K1, *P2, K4, P1, K1, P1, K4, P2, K22[26:26:30], rep from * once more, P2, K4, P1, K1, P1, K4, P2, K1.

24th row K1, *K2, P5, K1, P5, K2, P22[26:26:30], rep from * once more, K2, P5, K1, P5, K3.
These 24 rows form patt. Rep them once more.

3rd and 4th sizes only
Work 1st to 4th rows once more.

Shape shoulders (all sizes)
Working 1st and 2nd patt rows, cast off 20[22:22:24] sts at beg of next 2 rows.
Leave rem 51[55:55:59] sts on holder for centre neck.

Back yoke
With Rs of work facing, rejoin yarn to rem 103[109:115:121] sts on spare needle and K13 sts for second gusset and sl them on to a holder, K to end.
Complete back yoke to match front yoke.

Neck gusset
Join shoulder seams.
Sl front and back neck sts on to two No 9/3¾mm double ended needles.

Left side
With Rs of work facing, use another No 9/3¾mm needle, pick up and K one st from neck edge of shoulder seam, turn, P this st.
Next row K1, K1 from front neck sts, turn.
Next row P2, P1 from back neck sts, turn.
Next row K3, K1 from front neck sts, turn.
Cont in this way until there are 7 sts on needle. Break off yarn and leave sts for time being.

Right side
Work another neck gusset in same way, beg at right shoulder seam and reading back neck sts for front neck sts, and vice versa. Do not break off yarn.

Neckband
With Rs of work facing and set of four No 9/3¾mm needles, K across all sts round neck. 104[112:112:120] sts.
Place a contrast sl marker to denote beg of round.
1st round *K2, P2, rep from * to end.
Rep this round 11 times more, ending at sl marker.
With No 7/4½mm needle, cast off loosely in rib.

Sleeves
With Rs of work facing and set of four No 7/4½mm needles, K across 13 sts of one underarm

gusset, pick up and K75[75:83:83] sts evenly around rem armhole edge. 88[88:96:96] sts.
Place a contrast sl marker to denote beg of round.
1st round K13, P to end.
2nd round Sl 1, K1, psso, K9, K2 tog, P to end.
3rd round K to end.
4th round Sl 1, K1, psso, K7, K2 tog, K to end.
5th round K9, P to end.
6th round Sl 1, K1, psso, K5, K2 tog, P to end.
7th round K to end.
8th round Sl 1, K1, psso, K3, K2 tog, K to end.
9th round K to end.
10th round Sl 1, K1, psso, K1, K2 tog, K to end.
11th round K to end.

12th round Sl 1, K2 tog, psso, K to end.
13th round K to end.
14th round P1, K to end.
15th round K1, sl 1, K1, psso, K to last 2 sts, K2 tog.
16th round As 14th round.
17th round K to end.
18th and 19th rounds As 16th and 17th rounds.
20th round P1, sl 1, K1, psso, K to last 2 sts, K2 tog.
21st round K to end.
22nd round As 14th round.
23rd and 24th rounds As 13th and 14th rounds.
Rep the 15th to 24th rounds until 44[44:48:48] sts rem.
Cont without shaping, working a P st on every alt round as a mock seam st, until sleeve measures

16[16½:17:17½]in/41[42:43:44]cm from beg, or required length less 2in/5cm, ending at sl marker.

Cuff
Change to set of four No 9/3¾mm needles pointed at both ends.
Next round *K2, P2, rep from * to end.
Rep this round 11 times more.
Change to No 7/4½mm needle and cast off loosely in rib.

To make up
Press as directed on ball band, omitting ribbing.

Authentic guernsey

This traditional design for a man or woman features authentic guernsey patterns on the yoke, a slit garter stitch welt, underarm gussets, cast off shoulder ridges and a buttoned neckband. It is knitted in a guernsey 5 ply wool. To make the design simpler, it has been worked in separate sections and then seamed together.

Measurements

To fit 32 – 34[36 – 38:40 – 42]in/81 – 86[91 – 97:102 – 107]cm bust/chest
Actual measurements, 41[44:48]in/104[112:122]cm
Length to shoulders, 26½[28½:30½]in/67[73:77]cm
Sleeve seam, 17¾[19:20]in/45[48:51]cm
The figures in [] refer to the 36 – 38/91 – 97 and 40 – 42in/102 – 107cm sizes respectively

Materials

16[17:18] × 50g balls of Emu Guernsey 5 ply
One pair No 12/2¾mm needles
One pair No 11/3mm needles
One pair No 10/3¼mm needles
Cable needle
Set of four No 12/2¾mm needles pointed at both ends or No 12/2¾mm circular needle 60cm long
Two buttons
The quantities of yarn given are based on average requirements and are approximate

Tension

26 sts and 38 rows to 4in/10cm over st st worked on No 10/3¼mm needles

Cable pattern A

Worked over 8 sts.
1st row (Rs) K8 sts.
2nd row P8 sts.
3rd row Sl next 2 sts on to a cable needle and hold at back of work, K2 from left hand needle and then K2 from cable needle, sl next 2 sts on to a cable needle and hold at front of work, K2 from left hand needle then K2 from cable needle.

4th row P8 sts.
5th to 8th rows Rep 1st and 2nd rows twice.
These 8 rows form pattern A.

Diamond pattern B

Worked over 15 sts.
1st row (Rs) K7, P1, K7.
2nd and every foll alt row K all K sts and P all P sts as they appear, noting that this row will read P7, K1, P7.
3rd row K6, P1, K1, P1, K6.
5th row K5, (P1, K1) twice, P1, K5.
7th row K4, (P1, K1) 3 times, P1, K4.
9th row K3, (P1, K1) 4 times, P1, K3.
11th row K2, (P1, K1) 5 times, P1, K2.
13th row K1, (P1, K1) 7 times.
15th row As 11th row.
17th row As 9th row.
19th row As 7th row.
21st row As 5th row.
23rd row As 3rd row.
24th row As 2nd row.
These 24 rows form pattern B.

Back

With No 11/3mm needles cast on 124[136:148] sts. Work 20 rows g st, marking the ridge of the 1st row to denote Rs.
Next row (inc row) K8[9:11], *M1 by picking up loop lying between needles and K tbl, K12[13:14], rep from * 8 times more, M1, K8[10:11]. 134[146:158] sts.
Change to No 10/3¼mm needles.
1st row (Rs) K2, *P2, K2, rep from * to end.
2nd row P2, *K2, P2, rep from * to end.
These 2 rows form double rib patt. Rep them twice more.
Beg with a K row, cont in st st until back measures 16½[16¾:17½]in/42[44:46]cm from beg, ending with a P row.
Change to No 11/3mm needles.
Work 6 rows g st.
Change to No 10/3¼mm needles.
Commence yoke patt.
1st row (Rs) K7[3:9] sts, P2, (work 1st row cable patt A over next 8 sts, P2) 1[2:2] times, (work 1st row diamond patt B over next 15 sts, P2, work 1st row cable patt A over next 8 sts, P2) 4 times, (work 1st row cable patt A over next 8 sts, P2) 0[1:1] time more, K7[3:9] sts.
2nd row K9[5:11] sts, (work 2nd row cable patt A over next 8 sts, K2) 1[2:2] times, (work 2nd row diamond patt B over next 15 sts, K2, work 2nd row cable patt A over next 8 sts, K2) 4 times, (work 2nd row cable patt A over next 8 sts, K2) 0[1:1] time more, K7[3:9] sts.
Cont in patt as now set, rep 8 cable patt A rows and 24 diamond patt B rows, until back measures 26½[28½:30½]in/67[73:77]cm from beg, ending with a Ws row.
Leave sts on a spare needle.

Front

Work as given for back until front measures 24½[26¾:28¼]in/62[68:72]cm from beg, ending with a Ws row.

Shape neck

Next row Patt 56[60:64] sts, turn and leave rem sts on a spare needle.
Complete left shoulder first.
Cast off 2 sts at neck edge at beg of next and foll alt rows until 42[46:50] sts rem.
Cont without shaping until front measures same as back to shoulder, ending with same Ws patt row. Leave sts on a spare needle.
With Rs of work facing, sl first 22[26:30] sts from spare needle on to a holder for centre front neck, rejoin yarn to next st and patt 56[60:64] sts. Patt one row.
Complete right shoulder to match left, reversing shaping.

*Opposite: We picked a bright, bold red for this traditional 'gansey' which is knitted in separate sections. It features a garter stitch welt, slit at the side seams, a side-buttoned neckband and underarm gussets.
Designed by Jan Bird.*

Pattern pieces

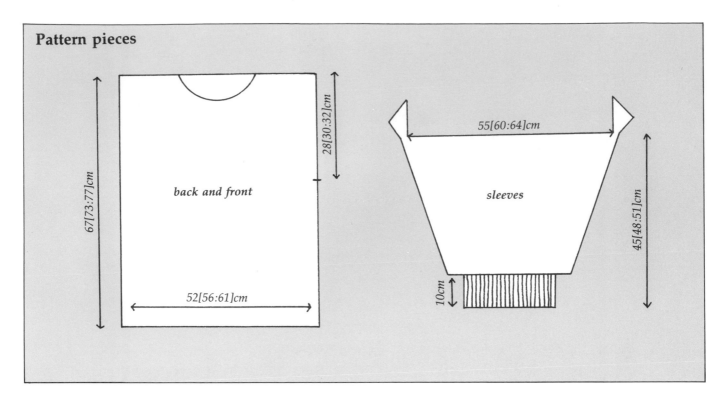

Diagram labels: back and front — 67[73:77]cm, 28[30:32]cm, 52[56:61]cm; sleeves — 55[60:64]cm, 45[48:51]cm, 10cm

Back and front shoulder seams

With Ws of back and front tog, cast off 42[46:50] sts from back and front spare needles *tog* to form ridged seam on Rs of work. Work other shoulder to match, leaving centre 50[54:58] sts on holder for back neck.

Sleeves

With No 12/2¾mm needles cast on 66[70:74] sts. Work 4in/10cm double rib as given for back, ending with a Rs row.
Next row (inc row) Rib 6[3:5] sts, *M1 as given for back, rib 6[7:7] sts, rep from * 8 times more, M1, rib 6[4:6] sts. 76[80:84] sts.
Change to No 10/3¼mm needles. Beg with a K row cont in st st, inc one st at each end of 3rd and every foll 3rd row until there are 144[156:166] sts.
Cont without shaping until sleeve measures 17¾[19:20]in/ 45[48:51]cm from beg, ending with a P row.

Shape gusset

1st row K1, inc in next st, K to last 2 sts, inc in next st, K1.

2nd row P to end.
3rd row K2, inc in next st, K to last 3 sts, inc in next st, K2.
4th row P to end.
5th row K3, inc in next st, K to last 4 sts, inc in next st, K3.
6th row P to end.
Cont inc in this way until 6 sts at each end have been inc, ending with an inc row.
Next row P to end.
Next row K7, *P2, K2, rep from * to last 9 sts, P2, K7.
Next row P7, *K2, P2, rep from * to last 9 sts, K2, P7.
Rep last 2 rows once more.
Next row K6 sts and leave on holder, cast off all but last 6 sts loosely, K6 sts.
Complete this side first.
Next row P4, P2 tog.
Next row K to end.
Next row P3, P2 tog.
Next row K to end.
Cont dec in this way until 2 sts rem. Work 2 tog and fasten off.
With Ws of work facing, rejoin yarn to 6 sts on holder and complete to match first side.

Neckband

With set of four No 12/2¾mm needles or circular needle, cast on

8 sts, K across sts on back neck holder, pick up and K27 sts down left side of front neck, K across front neck sts on holder, pick up and K27 sts up right front neck. 134[142:150] sts.
Work double rib in rows.
1st row P2, *K2, P2, rep from * to end.
2nd row K2, *P2, K2, rep from * to end.
Rep 1st row once more.
**Next row (buttonhole row) Rib to last 5 sts, yon, K2 tog, rib 3.
Work 5 more rows rib.**
Rep from ** to ** once more. Cast off in rib.

To make up

Press as directed on ball band, omitting ribbing and g st.
Sew down button band extension to inside of neckband.
Fold sleeves in half lengthways, with fold to shoulder seam, sew in place, sewing gusset to side edges.
Join side and sleeve seams, leaving g st welt open at sides
Sew on buttons to correspond with buttonholes.

Aran
knitting

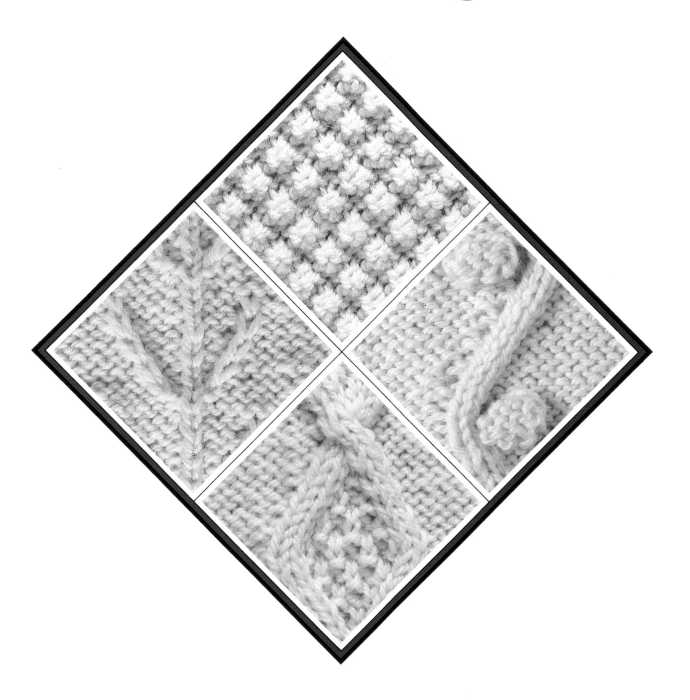

*The women of Ireland have always spun their own wool.
This multiple spinning wheel from Belleek, Co. Fermanagh, circa 1818,
was designed to allow four spinners to work simultaneously.*

Aran knitting

The mainland of Ireland is divided into four provinces. Northern Ireland is the province of Ulster and is made up of nine counties. The Republic of Ireland includes Leinster in the east which is divided into twelve counties, Munster in the south which has six counties and to the west lies Connacht with five counties, including Galway.

The west coast of Ireland faces into the bleak Atlantic and some thirty miles out into the Bay of Galway lie the three islands of Aran. The largest of these is Inishmore, then comes Inishmaan and the smallest is Inisheer. The terrain of all three islands is rugged and barren and life has always been hard for the inhabitants. For centuries the islanders cultivated the sparse covering of soil overlaying the hard rock surface, using seaweed to manure their crops and to provide fodder for their sturdy sheep and cattle.

The everyday language of the inhabitants is Gaelic and local songs and stories tell of the folklore and culture of the islands and the mainland. The women of Ireland have always spun their own wool and woven tweed for clothing but it is a frustrating exercise trying to trace the history of knitting because there are so few written records, or actual early examples. Early references to the life and traditions of the islanders mention that men often wore a woollen sweater under a waistcoat. This is described as grey or blue in colour and not the creamy-white we know today.

The most distinctive features of Aran knitting are the heavily-embossed fabrics and intricate patterns. It is claimed that this type of knitting has been known in the islands for many centuries but it was most likely based on Austrian and central European techniques, which would not have developed until quite a late date in the history of Aran knitting. Another early source of inspiration for these twisted, interlocked and encrusted patterns is said to be The Book of Kells but this seems most improbable, as this wonderfully illuminated manuscript of the Gospels of Matthew, Mark, Luke and John, believed to have been written between the sixth and eighth centuries, is one of Ireland's greatest treasures. It would only have been accessible to a very few privileged churchmen and it is unlikely that the inhabitants of the remote Aran islands would have had an opportunity of seeing the original manuscript. It is far more likely that the ancient Celtic crosses to be found all over the mainland of Ireland and the Aran islands were the original source of design for these highly-textured patterns.

The first real growth of the Aran knitting industry would probably have been as a direct result of the disastrous potato famines in Ireland in the mid and late nineteenth century. Government programmes encouraged all types of cottage industries in an endeavour to alleviate the appalling poverty and suffering, and knitting and crochet were developed throughout Ireland to provide a source of income. The women of Aran proved to be most adept at knitting, while the women of the mainland perfected the many forms of crochet we still practice today.

Aran knitting yarn also played its part in the character of Aran knitting, as the wool was spun and dyed locally. Mosses and seaweed gave soft, muted colours and the differences in each fleece gave a wide range of natural colours, through browns and greys to cream. The traditional name for Aran wool is 'bainin', pronounced 'bawneen', and this is the Irish word for undyed wool. It describes not so much the texture of the wool as the shade and today we regard cream as the authentic colour and it is the most popular choice for all types of Aran garments.

The stitch patterns in all folk knitting are often inspired by things in common to each area, such as local flora and fauna and the events in daily working life. Aran designs use many patterns featured in fishermens' ganseys and guernseys, but these have taken on local meanings. The shape of the traditional sweaters are classical and the whole emphasis is placed on the texture of the fabric, which had to be wind and weatherproof to withstand the often inhospitable climate.

The harsh and unspoilt way of life in the islands has altered dramatically in the past few decades, largely as a result of a thriving tourist industry and a planned revival of interest in the cottage crafts. Aran knitting has been particularly important in raising the standard of living and today there is a world-wide demand for these popular garments. We will never be able to trace the past history of the craft, but it is true to say that The Book of Kells and Celtic crosses have influenced Aran patterns in modern times and will probably continue to be a marvellous source of inspiration for these unique examples of hand-knitting in the future.

This section continues with the techniques used in some of the stitch patterns featured in Aran designs, together with row-by-row instructions for some traditional examples. The garments which follow have been designed to highlight authentic features, while still being practical for today's life-style.

Bobble patterns

Small, raised areas of knitting, which stand proud from the surface, are termed bobbles. These stitches are used extensively in Aran knitting and do much to give the fabric its characteristic three-dimensional appearance.

To work bobble stitches

The bobbles can be varied in size and in their position on the background fabric.

To make a small purl bobble against a stocking stitch background, work until the position for the bobble is reached. K1, P1, K1 all into the next stitch making three stitches out of one. Turn the needle, leaving the rest of the row unworked and knit these three stitches, then turn the needle again and purl three. To complete the bobble, use the point of the left hand needle to lift the second and third stitches over the top of the first stitch and off the needle, leaving the original stitch, (see Fig 1).

To make a large knit bobble against a reversed stocking stitch background, work until the position for the bobble is reached. Knit into the front and back of the next stitch twice, then into the front again, making five stitches out of one. Turn the needle, leaving the rest of the row unworked and purl these five stitches, then turn the needle again and knit five, then repeat these two rows so that you have worked the stitches four times. To complete the bobble, use the point of the left hand needle to lift the second, third, fourth and fifth stitches over the top of the first stitch and off the needle, leaving the original stitch, (see Fig 2).

fig 2 *completing a large bobble*

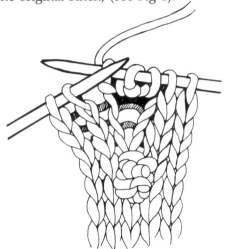

fig 1 *completing a small bobble*

Helping hand

When knitting a garment in a chunky weight, such as an Aran quality, seaming may be a problem. As a guide-line do not use a yarn thicker than a Double Knitting weight for seaming. If the knitting yarn is thicker, use a finer colour match.

The one area where neat seaming is essential is on the shoulder-line. The stepped effect of normal casting off in blocks of stitches is difficult to disguise. The following method gives a neat finish to all garments.

On a left front shoulder edge, or right back shoulder edge, when the point has been reached for the shoulder shaping, instead of casting off the required number of stitches at the beginning of the next knit row, on the *previous* purl row work to within this number of stitches, then turn the work. Slip the first stitch on the left hand needle then knit to the end of the row. Repeat this for the required number of rows, then purl across all the stitches on the last row. Cast off on the next knit row in the usual way, (see Fig 3).

On a right front shoulder edge, or left back shoulder edge, work as given above but reverse the shaping by beginning on a *knit* row.

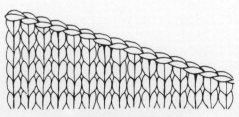

fig 3 *shaped casting off*

Traditional Aran patterns

Bobbles, cables and travelling stitches all play their part in the intricate patterns used in Aran knitting, and many of them have been given local names.

Trinity pattern

This simple stitch is also called blackberry pattern and its name derives from the method of working three stitches into one, and one stitch into three. It requires multiples of 4 stitches, plus 3, eg 19.

1st row (Rs) P to end.

2nd row K1, *(K1, P1, K1) into the next stitch, P3 tog, rep from * to the last 2 sts, (K1, P1, K1) into the next stitch, K1. Note that extra stitches have been increased in this row.

3rd row P to end.

4th row K1, *P3 tog, (K1, P1, K1) into the next stitch, rep from * to the last 4 sts, P3 tog, K1. Note that the stitches have now reverted to their original number. These 4 rows form the pattern.

Diamond panel

In this pattern two lines of travelling stitches worked in opposite directions are combined to form the diamond shape. The centre of each diamond is filled in with Irish moss stitch, a variation of single moss stitch worked over two rows instead of one. This sample has been worked as a panel over 14 stitches.

1st row (Rs) P5, K4, P5.

2nd and every foll alt row K all P sts of previous row and P all K sts; thus, this row will read K5, P4, K5.

3rd row P5, sl next 2 sts on to cable needle and hold at front of work, K2 from left hand needle then K2 from cable needle — called C4F —, P5.

5th row P4, sl next st on to cable needle and hold at back of work, K2 from left hand needle then K1 from cable needle — called Cr2R —, sl next 2 sts on to cable needle and hold at front of work, P1 from left hand needle then K2 from cable needle — called Cr2L —, P4.

7th row P3, Cr2R, P1, K1, Cr2L, P3.

9th row P2, Cr2R, (P1, K1) twice, Cr2L, P2.

11th row P1, Cr2R, (P1, K1) 3 times, Cr2L, P1.

13th row P1, Cr2L, (K1, P1) 3 times, Cr2R but work P1 from cable needle instead of K1, P1.

15th row P2, Cr2L, (K1, P1) twice, Cr2R as 13th row, P2.

17th row P3, Cr2L, K1, P1, Cr2R as 13th row, P3.

19th row P4, Cr2L, Cr2R as 13th row, P4.

20th row As 2nd row.

The 3rd to 20th rows form the pattern.

Zigzag and bobble panel

In this pattern two stitches travel across the fabric to form a zigzag line, with bobbles placed on either side of the zigzag. This sample has been worked as a panel over 14 stitches.

1st row (Rs) P3, K2, P9.

2nd and every foll alt row K all P sts of previous row and P all K sts: thus, this row will read K9, P2, K3.

3rd row P3, sl next 2 sts on to cable needle and hold at front of work, P1 from left hand needle then K2 from cable needle — called Cr2L —, P8.

5th row P4, Cr2L, P7.

7th row P5, Cr2L, P6.

9th row P6, Cr2L, P5.

11th row P7, Cr2L, P4.

13th row P5, (K into front and back of next st) twice then K into front again, (turn and K5, turn and P5) twice, use left hand needle to lift 2nd, 3rd, 4th and 5th sts over first st and off needle — called B1 —, P2, Cr2L, P3.

15th row P8, sl next st on to cable needle and hold at back of work, K2 from left hand needle then P1 from cable needle — called Cr2R —, P3.

17th row P7, Cr2R, P4.

19th row P6, Cr2R, P5.

21st row P5, Cr2R, P6.

23rd row P4, Cr2R, P7.

25th row P3, Cr2R, P2, B1, P5.

26th row As 2nd row.

The 3rd to 26th rows form the pattern.

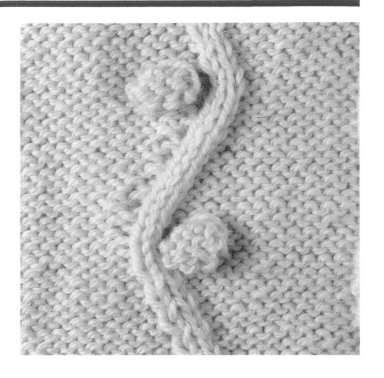

Tree of life pattern

Single lines of travelling stitches branch out from the central stitch to form this traditional pattern. To work as an all-over fabric this sample requires multiples of 15 stitches, or it can be worked as a single panel over 15 stitches.

1st row (Rs) *P7, K1, P7, rep from * in this and subsequent rows to form an all-over fabric.

2nd row *K7, P1, K7.

3rd row *P5, sl next st on to cable needle and hold at back of work, K1 from left hand needle then P1 from cable needle — called C2B —, K1 from left hand needle, sl next st on to cable needle and hold at front of work, P1 from left hand needle then K1 from cable needle — called C2F —, P5.

4th row *K5, sl 1 in a P-wise direction keeping yarn at front of work, K1, P1, K1, sl 1, K5.

5th row *P4, C2B, P1, K1, P1, C2F, P4.

6th row *K4, sl 1, K2, P1, K2, sl 1, K4.

7th row *P3, C2B, P2, K1, P2, C2F, P3.

8th row *K3, sl 1, K3, P1, K3, sl 1, K3.

9th row *P2, C2B, P3, K1, P3, C2F, P2.

10th row *K2, sl 1, K4, P1, K4, sl 1, K2.

These 10 rows form the pattern.

Opposite: Traditional Aran patterns have been incorporated into this design but the stitches are enhanced by the use of an Aran tweed yarn, (see pattern on page 55).
Designed by Pat Menchini.

Aran jersey with raglan sleeves

This design features traditional stitch patterns, such as Trinity stitch and honeycomb and is suitable for a man or a woman. The raglan sleeves make for ease-of-movement and the garment can be completed with a neat crew neck, or a snug polo collar.

Measurements

To fit 36[38:40:42]in/ 91[97:102:107]cm bust/chest
Actual measurements, 42[44:46:48]in/107[112:117:122]cm
Length to centre back neck, excluding neckband, 25½[26:26½:27]in/65[66:67:69]cm
Sleeve seam, 17[18:18½:18½]in/ 43[46:47:47]cm
The figures in [] refer to the 38/97, 40/102 and 42in/107cm sizes respectively

Materials

Round neck version, 21[21:22:22] × 50g balls of Sunbeam Aran Tweed
Polo neck version, 22[23:23:24] × 50g balls of same
One pair No 8/4mm needles
One pair No 6/5mm needles
Set of four No 8/4mm needles pointed at both ends
Cable needle
The quantities of yarn given are based on average requirements and are approximate

Tension

18 sts and 24 rows to 4in/10cm over st st worked on No 6/5mm needles

Left panel pattern

Worked over 17 sts.
1st row (Rs) K1, (sl next st on to cable needle and hold at back of work, K2 from left hand needle then P1 from cable needle — abbreviated as C1BP —, P3) twice, C1BP, K1.
2nd and every foll alt row Work across 17 sts K all K sts and P all P sts, noting that this row will read P1, (K1, P2, K3) twice, K1, P2, P1.
3rd row K1, sl next st on to cable needle and hold at back of work, K1 then P1 from cable needle, (P3, C1BP) twice, P1, K1.
5th row K1, P4, C1BP, P3, C1BP, P2, K1.
7th row K1, (P3, C1BP) twice, P3, K1.
9th row K1, P2, (C1BP, P3) twice, K2.
11th row K1, P1, (C1BP, P3) twice, sl next st on to cable needle and hold at back of work, K1 from left hand needle then K1 from cable needle — abbreviated as CB—, K1.
12th row As 2nd row.
These 12 rows form left panel.

Right panel pattern

Worked over 17 sts.
1st row (Rs) K1, (sl next 2 sts on to cable needle and hold at front of work, P1 from left hand needle then K2 from cable needle — abbreviated as C2FP —, P3) twice, C2FP, K1.
2nd and every foll alt row As 2nd row of left panel, noting that this row will read P1, (P2, K4) twice, P2, K1, P1.
3rd row K1, P1, (C2FP, P3) twice, sl next st on to cable needle and hold at front of work, P1 from left hand needle then K1 from cable needle, K1.
5th row K1, P2, (C2FP, P3) twice, P1, K1.
7th row K1, (P3, C2FP) twice, P3, K1.
9th row K2, (P3, C2FP) twice, P2, K1.
11th row K1, sl next st on to cable needle and hold at front of work, K1 from left hand needle then K1 from cable needle — abbreviated as CF —, (P3, C2FP) twice, P1, K1.

12th row As 2nd row.
These 12 rows form right panel.

Back

With No 8/4mm needles cast on 84[88:92:96] sts.
1st row (Rs) K3, *P2, K2, rep from * to last st, K1.
2nd row K1, *P2, K2, rep from * to last 3 sts, P2, K1.
Rep these 2 rows until back measures 3½in/9cm from beg, ending with a 2nd row.
Next row (inc row) Rib 0[2:4:6], (inc in next st, rib 1) 41 times, inc in next st, rib to end. 126[130:134:138] sts.
P one row.
Change to No 6/5mm needles. Commence patt.
1st row (Rs) K1, (P1, K1) 5[6:6:7] times, P2, (CF, CB) twice see 11th row of left and right panels for abbreviation, P2, work 1st row of left panel, P2, sl next 2 sts on to cable needle and hold at back of work, K1 from left hand needle then K2 from cable needle; now sl next st on to cable needle and hold at front of work, K2 from left hand needle then K1 from cable needle — abbreviated as C6 —, P2, K into back of next st — abbreviated as K1B —, P1, K1B, K20[20:24:24] sts, K1B, P1, K1B, P2, C6, P2, work 1st row of right panel, P2, (CF, CB) twice, P2, (K1, P1) 5[6:6:7] times, K1.
2nd row P11[13:13:15], K2, P8, K2, work 2nd row of right panel, K2, P6, K2, P into back of next st — abbreviated as P1B —, K1, P1B, (P3 tog, K1, P1, K1 all into next st to make 3) 5[5:6:6] times, P1B, K1, P1B, K2, P6, K2, work 2nd row of left panel, K2, P8, K2, P to end.
3rd row K1, (P1, K1)5[6:6:7] times, P2, (CB, CF) twice, P2, work 3rd row of left panel, P2, K6, P2, K1B, P1, K1B, P20[20:24:24], K1B, P1, K1B, P2, K6, P2, work 3rd row of right panel, P2, (CB, CF) twice, P2, (K1, P1) 5[6:6:7] times, K1.
4th row P11[13:13:15], K2, P8, K2, work 4th row of right panel, K2, P6, K2, P1B, K1, P1B, (K1, P1, K1 all into next st, P3 tog) 5[5:6:6] times, P1B, K1, P1B, K2, P6, K2,

Pattern pieces

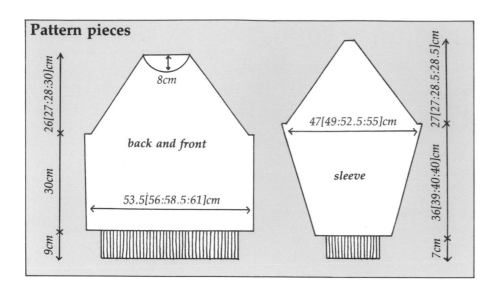

work 4th row of left panel, K2, P8, K2, P to end.
5th to 12th rows Rep 1st to 4th rows twice, but working 5th to 12th rows of left and right panels as now set.
These 12 rows form patt.
Cont in patt until back measures 15½in/39cm from beg, ending with a Ws row.

Shape raglans

Keep patt correct throughout.
1st row Cast off 2 sts, patt to end.
2nd row Cast off 2 sts, patt to end.
3rd row K1, K2 tog tbl, patt to last 3 sts, K2 tog, K1.
4th row K1, P1, patt to last 2 sts, P1, K1.
Rep 3rd and 4th rows until 98[102:98:102] sts rem, ending after a 4th row.
Next row As 3rd row.
Next row K1, P2 tog, patt to last 3 sts, P2 tog tbl, K1.
Rep last 2 rows until 30[30:34:34] sts rem.
Leave sts on holder for centre back neck.

Front

Work as given for back until 54[58:62:66] sts rem in raglan shaping, ending with a Ws row.

Shape neck

Next row K1, K2 tog tbl, patt 15[17:17:19] sts, turn and leave rem sts on a spare needle.
Complete left side first.
Cont dec at raglan edge on every row, *at the same time* dec one st at neck edge on next 4 rows.
9[11:11:13] sts.

Cont dec at raglan edge only until 2 sts rem.
Next row Work 2 tog. Fasten off.
With Rs of work facing, sl first 18[18:22:22] sts from spare needle on to a holder and leave for centre front neck, rejoin yarn to rem sts and with Rs facing, patt to last 3 sts, K2 tog, K1.
Complete right side to match left side.

Sleeves

With No 8/4mm needles cast on 36[40:40:44] sts. Work 3in/7cm rib as given for back welt, ending with a 2nd row.
Next row (inc row) Rib 1[5:3:7] sts, inc one st in each of next 33[29:33:29] sts, rib to end. 69[69:73:73] sts.
P one row.
Change to No 6/5mm needles.
Commence patt.
1st row (Rs) K1, (P1, K1) 1[1:2:2] times, P2, work 1st row of left panel, P2, C6, P2, (K1B, P1) 3 times, P1, C6, P2, work 1st row of right panel, P2, (K1, P1) 1[1:2:2] times, K1.
2nd row P3[3:5:5], K2, work 2nd row of right panel, K2, P6, K2, (P1B, K1) 3 times, K1, P6, K2, work 2nd row of left panel, K2, P to end.
3rd row K1, (P1, K1) 1[1:2:2] times, P2, work 3rd row of left panel, P2, K6, P2, (K1B, P1) 3 times, P1, K6, P2, work 3rd row of right panel, P2, (K1, P1) 1[1:2:2] times, K1.
4th row As 2nd row but working 4th row of left and right panels.
5th to 12th rows Rep 1st to 4th

rows twice, but working 5th to 12th rows of left and right panels. These 12 rows form patt.
Cont in patt, inc one st at each end of next and every foll 8th[6th:6th:4th] row until there are 81[87:87:79] sts, then on every foll 10th[8th:8th:6th] row until there are 85[89:95:99] sts, taking extra sts into broken rib patt.
Cont without shaping until sleeve measures 17[18:18½:18½]in/ 43[46:47:47]cm from beg, ending with a Ws row.

Shape raglan

1st to 4th rows Work as given for back raglan shaping.
Rep 3rd and 4th rows only until 37[41:45:49] sts rem, ending after a 4th row.
Next row As 3rd row.
Next row K1, P2 tog, patt to last 3 sts, P2 tog tbl, K1.
Rep last 2 rows until 9 sts rem. Sl sts on to a spare needle.

Neckband (optional)

Join back, front and sleeves raglan shapings.
**With Rs of work facing and set of four No 8/4mm needles, K across sts of back neck dec 3[3:5:5] sts evenly, K across sts of left sleeve top, pick up and K10[12:14:14] sts down left side of front neck, K across front neck sts on holder dec 3[3:5:5] sts evenly, pick up and K10[12:14:14] sts up right side of front neck and K across sts of right sleeve top. 80[84:92:92] sts. **
Work in rounds of K2, P2 rib for 1¼[1¼:1½:1½]in/3[3:4:4] cm.
Cast off loosely in rib.

Polo collar (optional)

Work as given for neckband from ** to **.
Work in rounds of K2, P2 rib for 6½[6½:7:7]in/17[17:18:18]cm.
Cast off loosely in rib.

To make up

Press as given on ball band, omitting ribbing.
Join side and sleeve seams. Press seams.

Aran jersey

All the traditions of Aran knitting are incorporated into this design, which is suitable for a man or a woman.
The stitch patterns and Aran wool are authentic and the jersey features a dropped shoulder-line and neat, round neck.

Measurements

To fit 35 – 37[39 – 42]in/89 – 94[99 – 107]cm bust/chest
Actual measurements, 41[46]in/ 104[117]cm
Length to shoulders, 24[26]in/ 61[67]cm
Sleeve seam, 18[19]in/46[48]cm
The figures in [] refer to the 39 – 42in/99 – 107cm size only

Materials

8[9] × 100g balls of Robin Aran 100
One pair No 8/4mm needles
One pair No 6/5mm needles
Cable needle
The quantities of yarn given are based on average requirements and are approximate

Tension

19 sts and 26 rows to 4in/10cm over panel patt A worked on No 6/5mm needles

Panel pattern A

Worked over 13[19] sts.
1st foundation row (Rs) P1, (K5, P1) 2[3] times.
2nd foundation row K1, (P5, K1) 2[3] times.
Now work in main patt.
1st row P1, (K5, P1) 2[3] times.
2nd row K13[19] sts.
3rd row P1, (K5, P1) 2[3] times.
4th row K1, (P5, K1) 2[3] times.
These 4 rows form panel patt A.
Note: When knitting sleeves, panel patt A is worked over 7 sts only and the figs in brackets are worked once.

Panel pattern B

Worked over 10 sts.
1st foundation row (Rs) P3, K1, P6.
2nd foundation row K6, P1, K3.
Now work in main patt.
1st row P1, (P1, K1, P1) all into next st making 3 sts from 1, turn, K3, turn, P3 then sl 2nd and 3rd sts over first st and off needle to complete bobble — abbreviated as MB —, P1, sl next st on to cable needle and hold at front of work, P1 from left hand needle then K1 from cable needle — abbreviated as C2L —, P5.
2nd row K5, P1, K4.
3rd row P4, C2L, P4.

4th row K4, P1, K5.
5th row P5, C2L, P3.
6th row K3, P1, K6.
7th row P6, C2L, P2.
8th row K2, P1, K7.
9th row P6, sl next st on to cable needle and hold at back of work, K1 from left hand needle then P1 from cable needle — abbreviated as C2R —, P1, MB.
10th row K3, P1, K6.
11th row P5, C2R, P3.
12th row K4, P1, K5.
13th row P4, C2R, P4.
14th row K5, P1, K4.
15th row P3, C2R, P5.
16th row K6, P1, K3.
These 16 rows form panel patt B.

Panel pattern C

Worked over 20 sts.
1st foundation row (Rs) (P2, K7) twice, P2.
2nd foundation row (K2, P7) twice, K2.
Now work in main patt.
1st row (P2, sl next 2 sts on to cable needle and hold at back of work, K1 from left hand needle then K2 from cable needle, K1, sl next st on to cable needle and hold at front of work, K2 from left hand needle then K1 from cable needle) twice, P2.
2nd row (K2, P7) twice, K2.
3rd row (P2, K7) twice, P2.

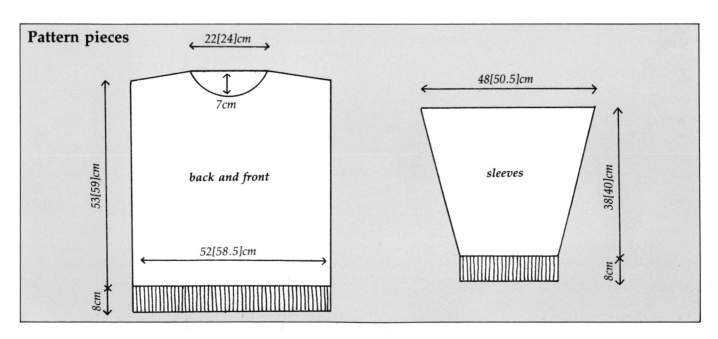

Pattern pieces

22[24]cm

7cm

53[59]cm

back and front

52[58.5]cm

8cm

48[50.5]cm

sleeves

38[40]cm

8cm

4th row (K2, P7) twice, K2.

These 4 rows form panel patt C.

Panel pattern D

Worked over 34 sts.

1st foundation row (Rs) (P4, K2) 5 times, P4.

2nd foundation row (K4, sl next st on to cable needle and hold at front of work, P1 from left hand needle then P1 from cable needle — abbreviated as Tw2P) 5 times, K4.

Now work in main patt.

1st row P3, (C2R, C2L, P2) 5 times, P1.

2nd row K3, (P1, K2) 10 times, K1.

3rd row P2, (C2R, P2, C2L) 5 times, P2.

4th row K2, P1, K4, (Tw2P, K4) 4 times, P1, K2.

5th row P2, (C2L, P2, C2R) 5 times, P2.

6th row K3, (P1, K2) 10 times, K1.

7th row P3, (C2L, C2R, P2) 5 times, P1.

8th row K4, (Tw2P, K4) 5 times.

These 8 rows form panel patt D.

Back

With No 8/4mm needles cast on 116[128] sts. Commence twisted rib for welt.

1st row (Rs) *K next st tbl, P1, rep from * to end.

Rep this row 18 times more.

Next row (inc row) Rib 24[30] sts, M1 by picking up loop lying between needles and K tbl, rib 15, M1, rib 38, M1, rib 15, M1, rib 24[30] sts. 120[132] sts.

Change to No 6/5mm needles. Commence patt placing patt panels as foll:

1st foundation row (Rs) Work 1st foundation row of panel patt A, work 1st foundation row of panel patt B, work 1st foundation row of panel patt C, work 1st foundation row of panel patt D, work 1st foundation row of panel patt C, work 1st foundation row of panel patt B and, finally, work 1st foundation row of panel patt A.

2nd foundation row Work 2nd foundation row panel patt A, work 2nd foundation row panel patt B, work 2nd foundation row panel patt C, work 2nd foundation row panel patt D, work 2nd foundation row panel patt C, work 2nd foundation row panel patt B

and, finally, work 2nd foundation row panel patt A.

Now work in main patt as foll:

1st row Work 1st row panel patt A, work 1st row panel patt B, work 1st row panel patt C, work 1st row panel patt D, work 1st row panel patt C, work 1st row panel patt B, work 1st row panel patt A.

Cont in patt as now set, working appropriate rows of each panel patt, until back measures 24[26½]in/61[67]cm from beg, ending with a Ws row.

Shape shoulders

Cast off 13[14] sts at beg of next 4 rows and 13[15] sts at beg of foll 2 rows.

Leave rem 42[46] sts on a holder for centre back neck.

Front

Work as given for back until front measures 21½[24]in/55[61]cm from beg, ending with a Ws row.

Shape neck

Keep patt correct throughout.

Next row Patt 49[53] sts, turn and leave rem sts on a spare needle. Complete left shoulder first.

Dec one st at neck edge on every row until 39[43] sts rem.

Cont without shaping until front measures same as back to shoulder, ending at side edge.

Shape shoulder

Cast off 13[14] sts at beg of next and foll alt row. Work one row. Cast off rem 13[15] sts.

With Rs of work facing, sl first 22[26] sts from spare needle on to holder and leave for centre front neck, rejoin yarn to rem sts and patt to end. 49[53] sts.

Complete right shoulder to match left shoulder, noting that an extra row will have to be worked before beg of shoulder shaping.

Sleeves

With No 8/4mm needles cast on 44 sts for both sizes. Work 17 rows twisted rib as given for back welt.

Next row (inc row) Rib 2, M1 as given for back, rib 2, M1, rib 36, M1, rib 2, M1, rib 2. 48 sts.

Change to No 6/5mm needles. Commence patt placing patt panels as foll:

1st foundation row (Rs) Work 7[7]

sts as 1st foundation row panel patt A, work 1st foundation row panel patt D, work 7[7] sts as 1st foundation row panel patt A.

2nd foundation row Work 7[7] sts as 2nd foundation row panel patt A, work 2nd foundation row panel patt D, work 7[7] sts as 2nd foundation row panel patt A.

Now work in main patt as foll:

1st row Work 7[7] sts as 1st row panel patt A, work 1st row panel patt D, work 7[7] sts as 1st row panel patt A.

Cont in patt as now set, working appropriate row of panels A and D for 3 rows. Cont in patt, inc one st at each end of next and every foll 4th row until there are 92[96] sts, working extra sts into panel patt A.

Cont without shaping until sleeve measures 18[19]in/46[48]cm from beg, ending with a Ws row.

Cast off loosely in patt.

Neckband

Join right shoulder seam.

With Rs of work facing and No 8/4mm needles, pick up and K20[20] sts down left side of front neck, K22[26] sts from front neck holder, pick up and K20[20] sts up right front neck then K42[46] sts from back neck holder. 104[112] sts.

Work 7 rows twisted rib as given for back welt.

Cast off in rib.

To make up

Do not press.

Join left shoulder and neckband seam.

Fold sleeves in half lengthways, with fold to shoulder seam, sew sleeves in place.

Join side and sleeve seams.

Opposite: The simple shape of this Aran jersey means that you can avoid complicated shaping when working the panels of authentic patterns. It has a neat, round neckline and dropped shoulders. Designed by Maureen Briggs.

Random dyed Aran jersey

This design has a dropped shoulder line and is suitable for a man or woman.
It is not as highly textured as some Aran garments but relies for effect on an unusual random-dyed yarn, which lifts it into the couture class.

Measurements

To fit 36[38:40:42:44]in/
91[97:102:107:112]cm bust/chest loosely
Actual measurements,
42[43½:46:47½:50½]in/
107[110:117:121:128]cm
Length to shoulders,
25½[26½:27:27¼:27½]in/
65[67:68:69:70]cm
Sleeve seam,
19[19½:19½:19½:19½]in/
48[49:49:49:49]cm
The figures in [] refer to the 38/97, 40/102, 42/107 and 44in/112cm sizes respectively

Materials

11[11:12:12:13] × 50g balls of Jaeger Prelude Peacocks Double Knitting
One pair No 10/3¼mm needles
One pair No 8/4mm needles
Cable needle
The quantities of yarn given are based on average requirements and are approximate

Tension

22 sts and 30 rows to 4in/10cm over st st worked on No 8/4mm needles

Panel pattern A

Worked over 22 sts.
1st row (Rs) P9, K4, P9.
2nd and every alt row K all K sts and P all P sts, noting that this row will read K9, P4, K9.
3rd row P7, sl next 2 sts on to a cable needle and hold at back of work, K2 from left hand needle then P2 from cable needle — abbreviated as Cr4BP —, sl next 2 sts on to a cable needle and hold at front of work, P2 from left hand needle then K2 from cable needle

— abbreviated as Cr4FP —, P7.
5th row P7, K2, P4, K2, P7.
7th row P5, Cr4BP, P4, Cr4FP, P5.
9th row P5, K2, P8, K2, P5.
11th row P3, Cr4BP, P8, Cr4FP, P3.
13th row P3, K2, P12, K2, P3.
15th row As 13th row.
17th row P3, Cr4FP, P8, Cr4BP, P3.
19th row As 9th row.
21st row P5, Cr4FP, P4, Cr4BP, P5.
23rd row As 5th row.
25th row P7, Cr4FP, Cr4BP, P7.
26th row As 2nd row.
These 26 rows form panel patt A.

Panel pattern B

Worked over 14 sts.
1st row (Rs) P3, K8, P3.
2nd and every alt row K all K sts and P all P sts, noting that this row will read K3, P8, K3.
3rd row P3, sl next 2 sts on to cable needle and hold at back of work, K2 from left hand needle then K2 from cable needle — abbreviated as C4B —, sl next 2 sts on to cable needle and hold at front of work, K2 from left hand needle then K2 from cable needle — called C4F —, P3.
5th, 7th and 9th rows As 1st row.
11th row P3, C4F, C4B, P3.
12th row As 2nd row.
These 12 rows form panel patt B.

Panel pattern C

Worked over 38 sts.
1st row (Rs) K tog next 2 sts on left hand needle but do not sl sts off needle, K the first of these 2 sts again and sl both sts off needle — abbreviated as Sp2F —, P12, K10, P12, Sp2F.
2nd row P2, K12, P10, K12, P2.
3rd row Sp2F, P12, K2, P1, K into back of next st — abbreviated as KB1 —, P2, KB1, P1, K2, P12, Sp2F.
4th row P2, K12, P2, K1, P into back of next st — abbreviated as PB1 —, K2, PB1, K1, P2, K12, P2.
5th row Sp2F, P10, Cr4BP (see 3rd row patt A), P1, KB1, P2, KB1, P1, Cr4FP (see 3rd row patt A), P10, Sp2F.

6th row P2, K10, P2, K3, PB1, K2, PB1, K3, P2, K10, P2.
7th row Sp2F, P10, K2, P3, KB1, P2, KB1, P3, K2, P10, Sp2F.
8th row As 6th row.
9th row Sp2F, P8, Cr4BP, (KB1, P2) 3 times, KB1, Cr4FP, P8, Sp2F.
10th row P2, K8, P2, (K2, PB1) 4 times, K2, 2, K8, P2.
11th row Sp2F, P8, K2, (P2, KB1) 4 times, P2, K2, P8, Sp2F.
12th row As 10th row.
13th row Sp2F, P6, Cr4BP, (P2, KB1) 4 times, P2, Cr4FP, P6, Sp2F.
14th row P2, K6, P2, K4, (PB1, K2) 4 times, K2, P2, K6, P2.
15th row Sp2F, P6, K2, P1, (KB1, P2) 5 times, KB1, P1, K2, P6, Sp2F.
16th row P2, K6, P2, K1, (PB1, P2) 5 times, PB1, K1, P2, K6, P2.
17th row Sp2F, P4, Cr4BP, P1, (KB1, P2) 5 times, KB1, P1, Cr4FP, P4, Sp2F.
18th row P2, K4, P2, K3, (PB1, K2) 5 times, PB1, K3, P2, K4, P2.
19th row Sp2F, P4, K2, P3, (KB1, P2) 5 times, KB1, P3, K2, P4, Sp2F.
20th row As 18th row.
21st row As 19th row.
22nd row As 18th row.
23rd row Sp2F, P34, Sp2F.
24th row P2, K34, P2.
These 24 rows form panel patt C.

Back

With No 10/3¼mm needles cast on 101[107:113:117:123] sts.
1st row (Rs) K1, *P1, K1, rep from * to end.
2nd row P1, *K1, P1, rep from * to end.
Rep these 2 rows until back measures 2¾in/7cm from beg, ending with a 1st row.

Opposite: Twisted stitches and cables have been used for this jersey, which has a round neckband and dropped shoulder-line. Whilst the patterns are traditional, an unusual effect is achieved by the use of a modern, random-dyed yarn. Designed by Debbie Jenkins.

Next row (inc row) Rib 7[4:2:4:2]
sts, *M1 by picking up loop lying
between needles and K tbl, rib
4[5:5:5:5], rep from * to last
6[3:1:3:1] sts, M1, rib to end.
124[128:136:140:148] sts.
Change to No 8/4mm needles.
Commence patt, placing patt
panels as foll:
1st row (Rs) P3[5:9:11:15] sts, Sp2F
(see 1st row patt C), work 1st row
panel patt A, Sp2F, work 1st row
panel patt B, work 1st row panel
patt C, work 1st row panel patt B,
Sp2F, work 1st row as panel patt
A, Sp2F, P to end.
2nd row K3[5:9:11:15] sts, P2,
work 2nd row as panel patt A, P2,
work 2nd row as panel patt B,
work 2nd row as panel patt C,
work 2nd row as panel patt B, P2,
work 2nd row as panel patt A, P2,
K to end.
Cont in patt as now set, working
appropriate rows of each panel
patt, until back measures
25½[26½:27:27¼:27½]in/
65[67:68:69:70]cm from beg,
ending with a Ws row.

Shape shoulders

Cast off 10[11:12:12:13] sts at beg
of next 6 rows, then 11[10:10:12:13]
sts at beg of foll 2 rows.
Leave rem 42[42:44:44:44] sts on a
spare needle for centre back neck.

Front

Work as given for back until front
measures 22[22:24:24:24] rows less
than back to shoulder, ending
with a Ws row.

Shape neck

Keep patt correct throughout.
Next row Patt 52[54:58:60:64] sts,
turn and leave rem sts on a spare
needle.
Complete left shoulder first.
Dec one st at beg of next row and
at same edge 5[5:7:7:7] times.
Work one row.
Dec one st at neck edge on next
and every foll alt row until
41[43:46:48:52] sts rem.
Work 4[4:6:6:6] rows without
shaping, ending with a Ws row.

Shape shoulder

Cast off 10[11:12:12:13] sts at beg
of next and foll 2 alt rows. Work
one row.
Cast off rem 11[10:10:12:13] sts.

Pattern pieces

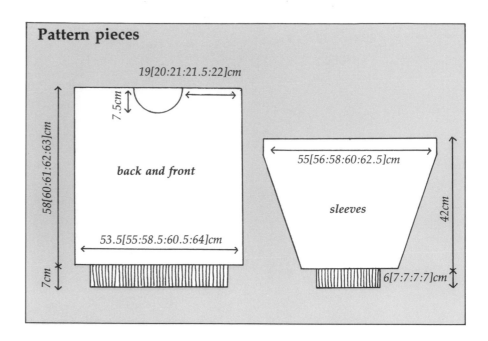

With Rs of work facing, sl first 20
sts from spare needle on to a
holder and leave for centre front
neck, rejoin yarn to rem sts and
patt to end.
Complete right shoulder to match
left, reversing all shapings and
noting that an extra row will have
to be worked before beg of
shoulder shaping.

Sleeves

With No 10/3¼mm needles cast on
55[55:55:57:57] sts. Work
2¼[2¾:2¾:2¾:2¾]in/6[7:7:7:7]cm
rib as given for back, ending with
a 1st row.
Next row (inc row) Rib 2[2:2:5:5]
sts, *M1 as given for back, rib 2,
rep from * to last 1[1:1:4:4] sts, M1,
rib to end. 82 sts.
Change to No 8/4mm needles.
Commence patt placing patt
panels as foll:
1st row (Rs) P4, Sp2F, P1, work 1st
row panel patt B, P1, work 1st row
panel patt C, P1, work 1st row
panel patt B, P1, Sp2F, P to end.
2nd row K4, P2, K1, work 2nd row
as panel patt B, K1, work 2nd row
as panel patt C, K1, work 2nd row
as panel patt B, K1, P2, K to end.
Cont in patt as now set, working
appropriate rows of each panel
patt, *at the same time* inc one st at
each end of 11th[5th:5th:5th:5th]
row from beg of patt and every foll
6th row until there are
120[120:112:104:92] sts, taking
extra sts into rev st st.

2nd, 3rd, 4th and 5th sizes only

Work 3 rows without shaping.
Inc one st at each end of next and
every foll 4th row until there are
[124:128:132:138] sts, taking extra
sts into rev st st.

All sizes

Work 7[5:5:5:5] rows, ending with
a Ws row.
Cast off loosely.

Neckband

Join right shoulder seam.
With Rs of work facing and No
10/3¼mm needles, pick up and
K18[18:22:22:22] sts down left side
of front neck, K20 sts from front
neck holder, pick up and
K18[18:22:22:22] sts up right front
neck, then K42[42:44:44:44] sts
from back neck holder, inc one st
in centre. 99[99:109:109:109] sts.
Beg and ending with a 2nd row,
work ¾in/2cm rib as given for
back.
Cast off in rib.

To make up

Do not press.
Join left shoulder and neckband
seam.
Fold sleeves in half lengthways,
with fold to shoulder seam, sew in
place.
Join side and sleeve seams.

Aran jackets

This comfortable jacket can be worked as a low-buttoning version for a woman, or a shawl-collared version for a man. It features a dropped shoulder-line and inset pockets on the fronts.

The yarn used for this design comes in a range of soft, muted colours, or you can use the traditional off-white shade.

Measurements

To fit 34 – 36[38 – 40:42 – 44]in/86 – 91[97 – 102:107 – 112]cm bust/chest

Actual measurements, 42[46:50]in/107[117:127]cm

Length to shoulders, 24½[26:27½]in/62[66:70]cm

Sleeve seam, 18[19:19]in/46[48:48]cm

The figures in [] refer to the 38 – 40/97 – 102 and 42 – 44/107 – 112cm sizes respectively

Materials

Low-buttoning version, 8[10:11] × 100g balls of Robin Aran 100

Shawl collared version, 9[10:11] balls of same

One pair No 8/4mm needles

One pair No 6/5mm needles

Cable needle

Four buttons

The quantities of yarn given are based on average requirements and are approximate

Tension

19 sts and 26 rows to 4in/10cm over panel patt A worked on No 6/5mm needles

Panel pattern A

Worked over multiples of 2 sts plus 1.

1st row (Rs) *P1, K1, rep from * to last st, P1.

2nd row *K1, P1, rep from * to last st, K1.

3rd row *K1, P1, rep from * to last st, K1.

4th row *P1, K1, rep from * to last st, P1.

These 4 rows form panel patt A.

Note: The number of sts in panel A will vary for the different panels

Panel pattern B

Worked over 37 sts.

1st row (Rs) P2, K4, P10, sl next st on to cable needle and hold at back of work, K1 tbl from left hand needle then P1 from cable needle — abbreviated as Tw2R —, K1, sl next st on to cable needle and hold at front of work, P1 from left hand needle then K1 tbl from cable needle — abbreviated as Tw2L —, P10, K4, P2.

2nd row K2, P4, K10, (P1, K1) twice, P1, K10, P4, K2.

3rd row P2, sl next 2 sts on to cable needle and hold at back of work, K2 from left hand needle then K2 from cable needle — abbreviated as C4B —, P9, Tw2R, K1, P1, K1, Tw2L, P9, sl next 2 sts on to cable needle and hold at front of work, K2 from left hand needle then K2 from cable needle — abbreviated as C4F —, P2.

4th row K2, P4, K9, (P1, K1) 3 times, P1, K9, P4, K2.

5th row P2, K4, P8, Tw2R, (K1, P1) twice, K1, Tw2L, P8, K4, P2.

6th row K2, P4, K8, (P1, K1) 4 times, P1, K8, P4, K2.

7th row P2, C4B, P7, Tw2R, (K1, P1) 3 times, K1, Tw2L, P7, C4F, P2.

8th row K2, P4, K7, (P1, K1) 5 times, P1, K7, P4, K2.

9th row P2, K4, P6, Tw2R, (K1, P1) 4 times, K1, Tw2L, P6, K4, P2.

10th row K2, P4, K6, (P1, K1) 6 times, P1, K6, P4, K2.

11th row P2, C4B, P5, Tw2R, (K1, P1) 5 times, K1, Tw2L, P5, C4F, P2.

12th row K2, P4, K5, (P1, K1) 7 times, P1, K5, P4, K2.

13th row P2, K4, P4, Tw2R, (K1, P1) 6 times, K1, Tw2L, P4, K4, P2.

14th row K2, P4, K4, (P1, K1) 8 times, P1, K4, P4, K2.

15th row P2, C4B, P3, Tw2R, (K1, P1) 7 times, K1, Tw2L, P3, C4F, P2.

16th row K2, P4, K3, (P1, K1) 9 times, P1, K3, P4, K2.

17th row P2, K4, P3, Tw2L, (P1, K1) 7 times, P1, Tw2R, P3, K4, P2.

18th row K2, P4, K4, (P1, K1) 8 times, P1, K4, P4, K2.

19th row P2, C4B, P4, Tw2L, (P1, K1) 6 times, P1, Tw2R, P4, C4F, P2.

20th row K2, P4, K5, (P1, K1) 7 times, P1, K5, P4, K2.

21st row P2, K4, P5, Tw2L, (P1, K1) 5 times, P1, Tw2R, P5, K4, P2.

22nd row K2, P4, K6, (P1, K1) 6 times, P1, K6, P4, K2.

23rd row P2, C4B, P6, Tw2L, (P1, K1) 4 times, P1, Tw2R, P6, C4F, P2.

24th row K2, P4, K7, (P1, K1) 5 times, P1, K7, P4, K2.

25th row P2, K4, P7, Tw2L, (P1, K1) 3 times, P1, Tw2R, P7, K4, P2.

26th row K2, P4, K8, (P1, K1) 4 times, P1, K8, P4, K2.

27th row P2, C4B, P8, Tw2L, (P1, K1) twice, P1, Tw2R, P8, C4F, P2.

28th row K2, P4, K9, (P1, K1) 3 times, P1, K9, P4, K2.

29th row P2, K4, P9, Tw2L, P1, K1, P1, Tw2R, P9, K4, P2.

30th row K2, P4, K10, (P1, K1) twice, P1, K10, P4, K2.

31st row P2, C4B, P10, Tw2L, P1, Tw2R, P10, C4F, P2.

32nd row K2, P4, K11, sl next 2 sts on to cable needle and hold at front of work, P1 from left hand needle, sl 2nd st on cable needle back on to left hand needle and K it, then P rem st on cable needle, K11, P4, K2.

These 32 rows form panel patt B.

Back

With No 8/4mm needles cast on 115[125:133] sts. Commence twisted rib.

1st row (Rs) K1 tbl — abbreviated as K1B —, *P1, K1B, rep from * to end.

2nd row P1, *K1B, P1, rep from * to end.

Rep these 2 rows 7[8:9] times more, then 1st row once more.

Next row (inc row) Rib 14[16:18] sts, *M1 by picking up loop lying between needles and K tbl, rib 29, M1, rib 29[35:39], M1, rib 29, M1, rib 14[16:18]. 119[129:137] sts. Change to No 6/5mm needles. Commence patt, placing patt panels as foll:

63

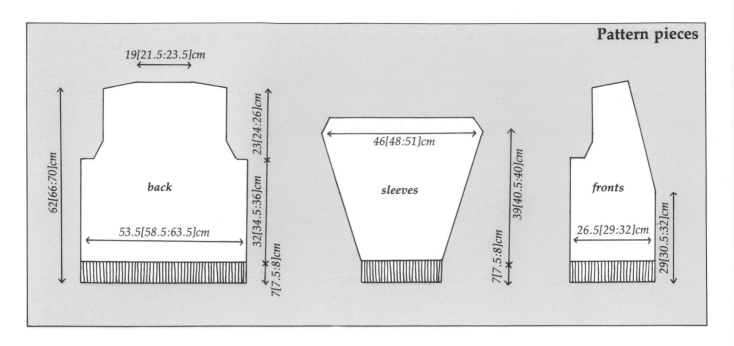

Pattern pieces

back — 19[21.5:23.5]cm, 62[66:70]cm, 23[24:26]cm, 32[34.5:36]cm, 53.5[58.5:63.5]cm, 7[7.5:8]cm

sleeves — 46[48:51]cm, 39[40.5:40]cm, 7[7.5:8]cm

fronts — 26.5[29:32]cm, 29[30.5:32]cm

1st row (Rs) Work 11[13:15] sts as 1st row panel patt A, work 1st row panel patt B, work 23[29:33] sts as 1st row panel patt A, work 1st row panel patt B, work 11[13:15] sts as 1st row panel patt A.

2nd row Work 11[13:15] sts as 2nd row of panel patt A, work 2nd row panel patt B, work 23[29:33] sts as 2nd row of panel patt A, work 2nd row panel patt B, work 11[13:15] sts as 2nd row panel patt A.

Cont in patt as now set, working appropriate rows of each panel patt, until back measures 15½[16½:17½]in/39[42:43]cm from beg, ending with a Ws row.

Shape armholes

Keeping patt correct throughout, cast off 5[6:7] sts at beg of next 2 rows, then dec one st at each end of next 4 Rs row. 101[109:115] sts. Cont without shaping in patt until armholes measure 9[9½:10]in/ 23[24:25]cm from beg of shaping, ending with a Ws row.

Shape shoulders

Cast off 11[11:11] sts at beg of next 4 rows, then 11[12:13] sts at beg of foll 2 rows.
Cast off rem 35[41:45] sts.

Pocket back (work 2)

With No 6/5mm needles cast on 25 sts for all sizes.
Work 22 rows in panel patt A.
Leave sts on holder for time being.

Left front

With No 8/4mm needles cast on 57[61:65] sts. Work 17[19:21] rows in twisted rib as given for back welt.

Next row (inc row) Rib 14[16:18] sts, M1 as given for back, rib 29, M1, rib 14[16:18] sts. 59[63:67] sts. Change to No 6/5mm needles. Commence patt, placing patt panels as foll:

1st row (Rs) Work 11[13:15] sts as 1st row of panel patt A, work 1st row panel patt B, work 11[13:15] sts as 1st row panel patt A.

2nd row Work 11[13:15] sts as 2nd row of panel patt A, work 2nd row of panel patt B, work 11[13:15] sts as 2nd row of panel patt A.

Cont in patt as now set, working appropriate rows of each panel patt until 24 patt rows have been worked.

Place pocket

Next row Work 11[13:15] sts of panel patt A, work first 6 sts of 25th row of panel patt B, sl next 25 sts on to a holder and leave for pocket top, in their place patt across 25 sts from pocket back, work last 6 sts of 25th row of panel patt B, work 11[13:15] sts of panel patt A.

Cont in patt without shaping until front measures 11½[12:12½]in/ 29[30:32]cm from beg, ending with a Ws row.

Shape front edge

Dec one st at front edge on next row and every foll 4th row until front measures same as back to underarm, ending at side edge.

Shape armhole

Cont dec at front edge on every 4th row as before, shape armhole by casting off 5[6:7] sts at beg of next row and dec one st at armhole edge on next 4 Rs rows. This completes armhole shaping. Cont to dec at front edge only on every 4th row until 33[34:35] sts rem.
Cont in patt without shaping until front measures same as back to shoulder, ending at armhole edge.

Shape shoulder

Cast off 11[11:11] sts at beg of next and foll alt row. Work one row then cast off rem 11[12:13] sts.

Right front

Work as given for left front, reversing all shaping.

Sleeves

With No 8/4mm needles cast on 41[45:49] sts. Work 17[19:21] rows twisted rib as given for back welt.
Next row (inc row) Rib 6[8:10] sts, M1 as given for back, rib 29, M1, rib 6[8:10] sts. 43[47:51] sts.
Change to No 6/5mm needles.
Commence patt, placing panel patts as foll:
1st row (Rs) Work 3[5:7] sts as 1st row of panel patt A, work 1st row panel patt B, work 3[5:7] sts as 1st row of panel patt A.
2nd row Work 3[5:7] sts as 2nd row of panel patt A, work 2nd row of panel patt B, work 3[5:7] sts as 2nd row of panel patt A.
Cont in patt as now set, working appropriate rows of each panel patt, *at the same time* inc one st at each end of next row and every foll 4th row until there are 87[91:95] sts, working extra sts into panel patt A.
Cont in patt without shaping until sleeve measures 18[19:19]in/ 46[48:48]cm from beg, ending with a Ws row.

Shape top

Place markers at each end of last row, then work 6[6:8] rows in patt without shaping.
Dec one st at each end of next 4 Rs

rows. Work one row without shaping.
Cast off loosely.

Shawl collar (optional)

Join shoulder seams.
With No 8/4mm needles cast on 11 sts for button band and collar. Work in twisted rib as given for back welt until band, when slightly stretched, fits up front edge to beg of front shaping, ending at inside edge. Pin in place.

Shape collar

Cont in twisted rib, inc one st at beg of next and every foll 4th row until there are 31[33:35] sts, working extra sts into twisted rib.
Cont without shaping until collar, when slightly stretched, fits up shaped front edge and round to centre back neck. Cast off.
Sew band and collar in position.
Mark 4 button position on button band, first to come 2 rows above cast on edge and 4th to come 2 rows below beg of front shaping, with 2 more equally spaced between.
Work buttonhole band and collar as given for button band, making buttonholes as markers are reached as foll:
1st buttonhole row (Rs) Rib 4, cast off 3 sts, rib to end.
2nd buttonhole row Rib 4, cast on 3 sts, rib to end.

Ribbed front bands (optional)

Work as given for button and buttonhole bands on shawl collar version from ** to **, then cont without shaping until band fits up front shaping and round to centre back neck. Cast off.
Sew bands in position.

Pocket tops (make 2)

With Rs of work facing and No 8/4mm needles, P1, (K1B, P1) 12 times across 25 sts of pocket tops on holders.
Work 5 rows in twisted rib. Cast off in rib.

To make up

Do not press.
Set in sleeves, sewing row ends above markers on sleeves to the sts cast off for armholes on back and fronts.
Join side and sleeve seams.
Sew down pocket backs to Ws, then catch down row ends of pocket tops.
Join cast off edges of collar or bands at centre back neck.
Sew on buttons.

Shetland lace knitting

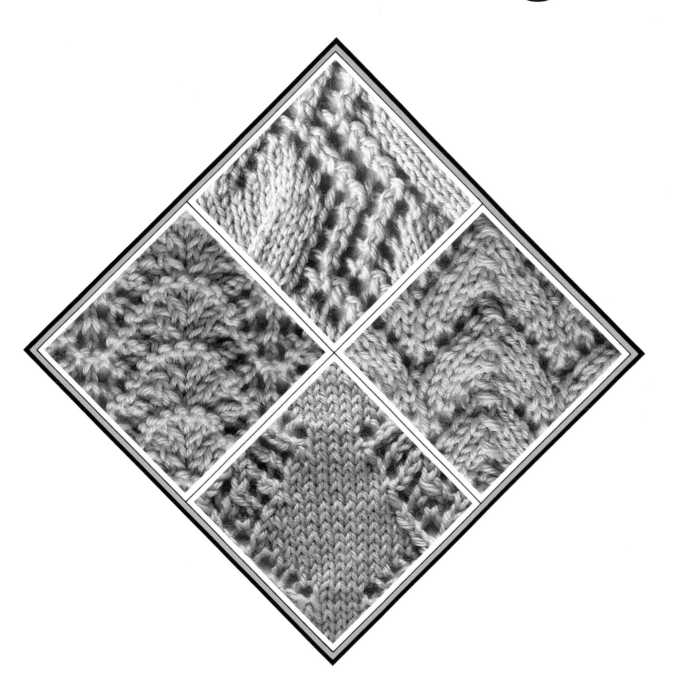

*This very early photograph shows knitters from the Shetlands dressing
gossamer fine shawls after they had been washed.
The shawls were laced on to large wooden frames
and left to dry out naturally.*

Shetland lace knitting

Shetland knitters are as famous for their superb lace knitting as they are for their instantly recognizable coloured patterns, and when the lace technique is combined with coloured stripes, the effects are quite magical.

We do not know where this form of lace knitting first originated but the technique was already well-established in Spain during the fourteenth century. It could well be that this form of island knitting stems from the Spanish knitted lace patterns, which came to the islands via established trading routes.

A later source of lace design could also have been based on needlepoint and pillow laces. Traditional Shetland lace knitting seems to have begun in the early nineteenth century and about this time, Mrs. Jessie Scanlon, an avid collector of Brussels, Valencia and Madeira laces, took examples from her collection with her, when she visited the Shetland Isles. It is recorded that the Shetland knitters were inspired to copy the lace and adapt it to hand knitted stitch patterns. This initial inspiration has gradually evolved into the distinctive fabric we know today, which is unique throughout the world.

The growth of lace knitting as a cottage industry in the islands was rapid but it was not a great commercial success, probably because the spinning of the yarn, to say nothing of the knitting, did not make it a viable proposition. It is said that the hand spinners could produce sufficient yarn from two ounces of fleece to knit a shawl almost 72in/158cm square! These exquisite Shetland shawls were so fine that they could easily be pulled through a wedding ring and they became known as 'wedding ring shawls'. They had the appearance of a gossamer spider's web, with no harsh beginning or ending, and would originally be worn as a bridal veil and then used for christenings. This fashion for fine knitted lace lasted barely sixty years and despite attempts to revive it, as the Edwardian age dawned so the demand waned. As with all forms of traditional knitting, the introduction of machine spinning and lace production, at very low prices, meant that hand spinning and knitting could no longer compete, in spite of the disparity in quality.

During its brief heyday, one of the reasons for the success of Shetland lace knitting would have been the quality of the wool used. The sheep bred in the islands are sturdy, hardy creatures, well able to resist disease and they have been on the islands since the Stone Age. The wool they produce becomes loose in the summer as a new fleece grows, so they do not need to be sheared and the wool can be plucked by hand. This means that it has a long staple, with no cut ends, and is exceptionally fine and soft.

Once a shawl of this delicacy had been completed, it was washed and dressed in the traditional manner. To do this, a special wooden frame as large as a bed was needed. The shawl was laced to the frame through every point on the edges of the border, and then left to dry out naturally. With this method, the shawl was kept square and taut and each scallop of the border would be stretched into shape. I know a designer of Shetland lace today who dresses shawls and scarves by pinning them out between layers of tissue paper and placing them under a carpet! Unorthodox maybe, but it works.

The traditional lace stitch patterns are few in number and only ten are considered to be truly authentic, although many more are termed as 'lace' patterns. Each stitch has been adapted to represent the natural beauty of these remote islands and they carry such evocative names as 'Old shale—or shell', 'Print o' the wave', 'Fern' and 'Horseshoe print'.

The most northerly island of Unst produced some of the finest examples of knitted lace during its brief spell of popularity. A few skilled knitters still remain in the Shetlands today, to carry on this tradition. Wedding ring shawls are still produced but as they can take up to a year to complete, they are almost beyond price. The islanders knit from huge charts, instead of row-by-row instructions as we do in commercial patterns today. The designs are so intricate and the stitch patterns so lengthy that they cannot economically be reproduced in magazine or book form to popularize them. The needles used to knit these shawls are still known today by their traditional name of 'wires', and this term gives us some indication of their fineness.

Even today, however, knitting in the authentic one ply is very rare and reminders of the past glories of lace knitting are either highly-prized heirlooms, or museum items. We can still experience some of the pride and pleasure in this technique, however, using modern yarns and row-by-row instructions. This section continues with instructions for some of the treasured stitch patterns and the garments that follow have been designed to meet today's requirements.

Traditional Shetland lace patterns

These patterns all use the decorative methods of increasing shown on page 134, to produce a motif formed by eyelet holes in the fabric. The increased stitches are compensated for at a later stage in the same pattern row, or in a following row.

A wonderful effect can be obtained by working these patterns in narrow stripes of contrasting colours, instead of a single colour throughout.

Old shale (or shell) pattern

There are many different versions of this beautiful scalloped pattern. It can be worked over varying multiples of stitches and the right side of the fabric can be in smooth stocking stitch, or broken with a knit ridge as this example. It requires multiples of 17 stitches, plus 2, eg 36.

1st row (Rs) K to end.
2nd row P to end.
3rd row K1, *(K2 tog) 3 times, (yfwd, K1) 5 times, yfwd, (sl 1, K1, psso) 3 times, rep from * to last st, K1.
4th row As 2nd row.
5th row As 3rd row.
6th row K to end.
These 6 rows form the pattern.

Horseshoe print pattern

This stitch is derived from the imprint of horseshoes on wet sand. It requires multiples of 10 stitches, plus 1, eg 31.

1st row (Ws) P to end.
2nd row K1, *yfwd, K3, sl 1, K2 tog, psso, K3, yfwd, K1, rep from * to the end.
3rd row As 1st row.
4th row P1, *K1, yfwd, K2, sl 1, K2 tog, psso, K2, yfwd, K1, P1, rep from * to the end.
5th row K1, *P9, K1, rep from * to the end.
6th row P1, *K2, yfwd, K1, sl 1, K2 tog, psso, K1, yfwd, K2, P1, rep from * to the end.
7th row As 5th row.
8th row P1, *K3, yfwd, sl 1, K2 tog, psso, yfwd, K3, P1, rep from * to the end.
These 8 rows form the pattern.

Fern pattern

This forms the shape of a fern motif worked in eyelet holes against a stocking stitch background. It was often used as a border on a wedding ring shawl. It requires multiples of 15 stitches, eg 30.

1st row (Rs) *K7, yfwd, sl 1 in a knitwise direction — called sl 1 —, K1, psso, K6, rep from * to the end.
2nd, 4th, 6th, 8th and 10th rows P to end.
3rd row *K5, K2 tog, yfwd, K1, yfwd, sl 1, K1, psso, K5, rep from * to the end.
5th row *K4, K2 tog, yfwd, K3, yfwd, sl 1, K1, psso, K4, rep from * to the end.
7th row *K4, yfwd, sl 1, K1, psso, yfwd, sl 1, K2 tog, psso, yfwd, K2 tog, yfwd, K4, rep from * to the end.
9th row *K2, K2 tog, yfwd, K1, yfwd, sl 1, K1, psso, K1, K2 tog, yfwd, K1, yfwd, sl 1, K1, psso, K2, rep from * to the end.
11th row *K2, (yfwd, sl 1, K1, psso) twice, K3, (K2 tog, yfwd) twice, K2, rep from * to end.
12th row *P3, (yrn, P2 tog) twice, P1, (P2 tog tbl, yrn) twice, P3, rep from * to the end.
13th row As 7th row.
14th row *P5, yrn, P2 tog, P1, P2 tog tbl, yrn, P5, rep from * to the end.
15th row *K6, yfwd, sl 1, K2 tog, psso, yfwd, K6, rep from * to the end.
16th row As 2nd row.
These 16 rows form the pattern.

Print o' the wave pattern

This gently undulating pattern is a reminder that the sea is a vital part of the life of the islands. It requires multiples of 22 stitches, plus 3, eg 47.

1st row (Rs) K4, *K2 tog, K3, (yfwd, K2 tog) twice, yfwd, K13, rep from * to the end, ending last rep with K12 instead of K13.
2nd and every foll alt row P to end.
3rd row K3, *K2 tog, K3, yfwd, K1, yfwd, (sl 1, K1, psso, yfwd) twice, K3, sl 1, K1, psso, K7, rep from * to the end.
5th row K2, *K2 tog, (K3, yfwd) twice, (sl 1, K1, psso, yfwd) twice, K3, sl 1, K1, psso, K5, rep from * to the last st, K1.
7th row K1, *K2 tog, K3, yfwd, K5, yfwd, (sl 1, K1, psso, yfwd) twice, K3, sl 1, K1, psso, K3, rep from * to the last 2 sts, K2.
9th row *K12, yfwd, (sl 1, K1, psso, yfwd) twice, K3, sl 1, K1, psso, K1, rep from * to the last 3 sts, K3.
11th row *K7, K2 tog, K3, (yfwd, K2 tog) twice, yfwd, K1, yfwd, K3, sl 1, K1, psso, rep from * to the last 3 sts, K3.
13th row K6, *K2 tog, K3, (yfwd, K2 tog) twice, (yfwd, K3) twice, sl 1, K1, psso, K5, rep from * to the end, ending last rep with K2 instead of K5.
15th row K5, *K2 tog, K3, (yfwd, K2 tog) twice, yfwd, K5, yfwd, K3, sl 1, K1, psso, K3, rep from * to the end, ending last rep with K1 instead of K3.
16th row As 2nd row.
These 16 rows form the pattern.

Shetland lace jersey

This beautiful jersey combines an authentic Shetland stitch pattern with narrow stripes of contrasting colours.
The design features a 'grand-dad' opening at the front neck and is in one size only.

Measurements

To fit 35 – 37in/89 – 94cm bust loosely
Actual measurements, 40in/102cm
Length to shoulder, 23½in/60cm
Sleeve seam, 18in/45cm

Materials

5 × 50g balls of Robin Landscape 4 ply in main shade A
1 × 50g ball of same in each of four contrasting colours, B, C, D and E
One pair No 12/2¾mm needles
One pair No 9/3¾mm needles
4 buttons
The quantities of yarn given are based on average requirements and are approximate

Tension

26 sts and 32 rows to 4in/10cm over patt worked on No 9/3¾mm needles

Back

With No 12/2¾mm needles and A, cast on 131 sts.
1st row (Rs) K1, *P1, K1, rep from * to end.
2nd row P1, *K1, P1, rep from * to end.
Rep these 2 rows until back measures 2¼in/6cm from beg, ending with a 2nd row.
Change to No 9/3¾mm needles.
Work foundation rows of patt.
1st foundation row K1, *yfwd, K3, sl 1, K2 tog, psso, K3, yfwd, K1, rep from * to end.
2nd foundation row P to end.
3rd foundation row P1, *K1, yfwd, K2, sl 1, K2 tog, psso, K2, yfwd, K1, P1, rep from * to end.
4th foundation row K1, *P9, K1, rep from * to end.
5th foundation row P1, *K2, yfwd,

K1, sl 1, K2 tog, psso, K1, yfwd, K2, P1, rep from * to end.
6th foundation row K1, *P9, K1, rep from * to end.
Commence main patt.
1st row (Rs) P1, *K3, yfwd, sl 1, K2 tog, psso, yfwd, K3, P1, rep from * to end.
2nd row P to end.
3rd row K1, *yfwd, K3, sl 1, K2 tog, psso, K3, yfwd, K1, rep from * to end.
4th row P to end.
5th row P1, *K1, yfwd, K2, sl 1, K2 tog, psso, K2, yfwd, K1, P1, rep from * to end.
6th row K1, *P9, K1, rep from * to end.
7th row P1, *K2, yfwd, K1, sl 1, K2 tog, psso, K1, yfwd, K2, P1, rep from * to end.
8th row K1, *P9, K1, rep from * to end.
These 8 rows form the main patt.
Cont. in 24-row striped patt as foll:
1st to 8th rows As 1st to 8th patt rows, working 1st and 2nd rows with B, 3rd and 4th rows with C, 5th and 6th rows with D and 7th and 8th rows with E.
9th to 24th rows With A, rep 1st to 8th patt rows twice.
Rep these 24 rows until back measures 15½in/40cm from beg, ending with 6 rows in A, and a Ws row.

Shape armholes

Keeping patt correct throughout, cast off 6 sts at beg of next 2 rows, then dec one st at each end of next and foll 3 alt rows. 111 sts.
Cont without shaping until armholes measure 8in/20cm from beg of shaping, ending with a Ws row.

Shape shoulders

Cast off 10 sts at beg of next 4 rows and 14 sts at beg of next 2 rows.
Leave rem 43 sts on a holder for centre back neck.

Front

Work as given for back until armhole shaping has been completed, ending with a 7th patt row. 111 sts.

Shape front opening

Next row Keeping patt correct throughout, patt 51 sts, leave these sts on a spare needle, cast off next 9 sts, patt to end.
Complete left front shoulder on these 51 sts.
Cont without shaping until armhole measures 5½in/14cm from beg of shaping, ending at neck edge.

Shape neck

Cast off 7 sts at beg of next row then dec one st at neck edge on next 10 rows. 34 sts.
Cont without shaping until front measures same as back to shoulder, ending at armhole edge.

Shape shoulder

Cast off 10 sts at beg of next and foll alt row. Work one row. Cast off rem 14 sts.
With Rs of work facing, rejoin yarn to rem sts and patt to end.
Complete right front shoulder to match left, reversing all shaping.

Sleeves

With No 12/2¾mm needles and A, cast on 55 sts and work 2¼in/6cm rib as given for back welt, ending with a Ws row.
Next row (inc row) Rib 5, *M1 by picking up loop lying between needles and K tbl, rib 9, rep from * to last 5 sts, M1, rib to end. 61 sts.
Change to No 9/3¾mm needles and work 6 foundation rows as given for back.
Work in main patt and same stripe sequence as given for back, inc one st at each end of next and every foll 5th row until there are 101 sts, working extra sts in st st until there are sufficient to bring them into patt.
Cont without shaping until sleeve measures 18in/46cm from beg, ending with 6 rows in A.

Opposite: Traditional Shetland horseshoe pattern, worked in broad stripes of the main colour and narrow stripes of contrasting colours, has been used for this very feminine jersey.
Designed by Maureen Briggs.

Place a marker at both ends of last row.
Work 8 rows in patt without shaping.

Shape top
Cast off 8 sts at beg of next 8 rows.
Cast off rem 37 sts.

Neckband
Join shoulder seams.
With Rs of work facing, No 12/ 2¾mm needles and A, pick up and K30 sts up right side of front neck, K across 43 sts on back neck holder and pick up and K30 sts down left side of front neck. 103sts.

Beg with a 2nd row, work 7 rows rib as given for back welt.
Cast off in rib.

Button band
With Rs of work facing, No 12/ 2¾mm needles and A, pick up and K44 sts down left side of front neck opening.
Work 11 rows K1, P1 rib.
Cast off in rib.

Buttonhole band
With Rs of work facing, No 12/ 2¾mm needles and A, pick up and K44 sts up right side of front neck opening.
Work 5 rows K1, P1, rib.
Next row (buttonhole row) Rib 10, *yrn, P2 tog, rib 8, rep from * to last 4 sts, yrn, P2 tog, rib 2.
Work 5 rows rib.
Cast off in rib.

To make up
Press as directed on ball band, omitting ribbing.
Set in sleeves, sewing the row ends above markers to the cast off armhole sts on back and front.
Join side and sleeve seams.
Catch down base of button and buttonhole bands to Ws. Sew on buttons.

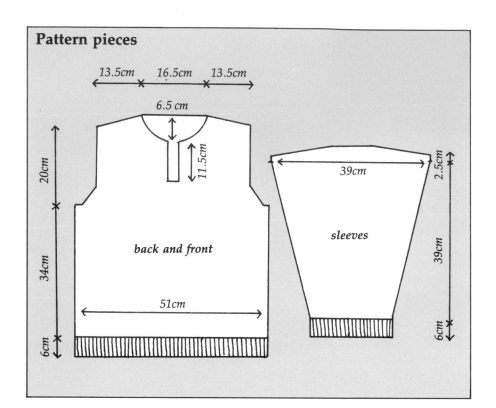

Pattern pieces

13.5cm 16.5cm 13.5cm

6.5 cm

11.5cm

20cm

34cm

6cm

51cm

back and front

39cm

2.5cm

39cm

6cm

sleeves

Helping hand
When using a very fine yarn and traditional lace patterns, harsh edges caused by the normal methods of casting on and off must be avoided.

The simplest way to avoid this when casting off is to use a needle two sizes larger than the size used for the main fabric and cast off in the usual way.

To work a looser version of the two needle method of casting on, instead of inserting the right hand needle *between* the last two stitches of the left hand needle to make another stitch, actually insert it *into* the last stitch on the left hand needle, (see Fig 1).

If lace fabric has to be joined, it is best to use a spare length of contrasting yarn for the loose method of casting on explained above. When the knitting is completed, this contrasting yarn can be removed, exposing the loops and allowing the first row to be grafted to the last row of the second piece, (see Fig 2).

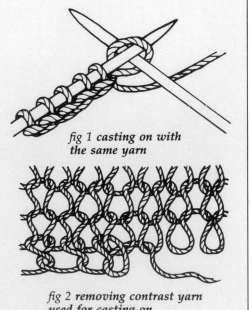

fig 1 casting on with the same yarn

fig 2 removing contrast yarn used for casting on

Cardigan in lace pattern

This button-to-the-neck cardigan is worked in candlelight pattern and a Shetland double knitting quality.
The design has a dropped shoulder line and neat round neck.

Measurements

To fit 34–36[38–40]in/86–91[97–102]cm bust
Actual measurements, 42[46]in/107[117]cm
Length to shoulders, 24½[26]in/62[66]cm
Sleeve seam, 15½[17]in/39.5[43]cm
The figures in [] refer to the 38–40in/97–102cm size only

Materials

10[11] × 50g balls of Wendy Shetland Double Knitting
One pair No 10/3¼mm needles
One pair No 8/4mm needles
Ten small buttons
The quantities of yarn given are based on average requirements and are approximate

Tension

23 sts and 30 rows to 4in/10cm over patt worked on No 8/4mm needles

Note

When dec in patt remember that every time an eyelet hole patt inc is eliminated its corresponding dec must also be eliminated.
When inc in patt remember not to work a new eyelet hole patt inc until you have also added enough sts to work its corresponding dec

Back

With No 10/3¼mm needles cast on 120[144] sts. Work in twisted rib for welt.
1st row *K1 tbl, P1, rep from * to end.
2nd row As 1st row.
Rep these 2 rows 8 times more, then 1st row once more.
Next row (inc row) K1 tbl, M1 by picking up loop lying between needles and K tbl, (P1, K1 tbl) 29[35] times, P1, M1, rib to last st, M1, P1. 123[147] sts.
Change to No 8/4mm needles.
Commence patt.
1st row (Rs) K1, *K1, yfwd, sl 1, K1, psso, K7, K2 tog, yfwd, rep from * to last 2 sts, K2.
2nd and every foll alt row K1, P to last st, K1.
3rd row K1, *K1, yfwd, K1, sl 1, K1, psso, K5, K2 tog, K1, yfwd, rep from * to last 2 sts, K2.
5th row K1, *K1, yfwd, K2, sl 1, K1, psso, K2, K2 tog, K2, yfwd, rep from * to last 2 sts, K2.
7th row K1, *K1, yfwd, K3, sl 1, K1, psso, K1, K2 tog, K3, yfwd, rep from * to last 2 sts, K2.
9th row K1, *K1, yfwd, K4, sl 1, K2 tog, psso, K4, yfwd, rep from * to last 2 sts, K2.
11th row K1, *K4, K2 tog, yfwd, K1, yfwd, sl 1, K1, psso, K3, rep from * to last 2 sts, K2.
13th row K1, *K3, K2 tog, K1, (yfwd, K1) twice, sl 1, K1, psso, K2, rep from * to last 2 sts, K2.
15th row K1, *K2, K2 tog, K2, yfwd, K1, yfwd, K2, sl 1, K1, psso, K1, rep from * to last 2 sts, K2.

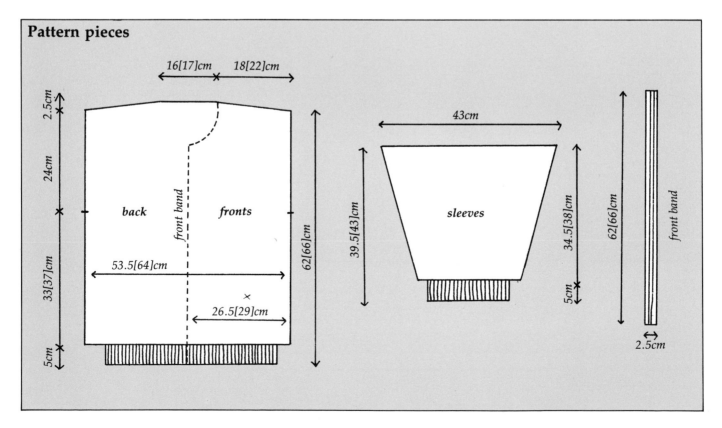

Pattern pieces

16[17]cm   18[22]cm

2.5cm
24cm
back   front band   fronts
53.5[64]cm
33[37]cm
26.5[29]cm
5cm
62[66]cm

39.5[43]cm
43cm
sleeves
34.5[38]cm
5cm

62[66]cm
front band
2.5cm

17th row K1, *K1, K2 tog, K3, yfwd, K1, yfwd, K3, sl 1, K1, psso, rep from * to last 2 sts, K2.
19th row K1, K2 tog, *K4, yfwd, K1, yfwd, K4, sl 1, K2 tog, psso, rep from * to last 12 sts, K4, yfwd, K1, yfwd, K4, sl 1, K1, psso, K1.
20th row As 2nd row.
These 20 rows form the patt.
Cont in patt until back measures 15[16½]in/38[42]cm from beg, (approx 100[110] patt rows), ending with a Ws row.
Mark each end of next row with contrast coloured threads to denote beg of armholes.
Cont without shaping until back measures 24½[26]in/62[66]cm from beg, (approx 70 more patt rows), ending with a 12th or 2nd row.

Shape shoulders

Keeping patt correct throughout, cast off 11[13] sts at beg of next 6 rows, and 10[14] sts at beg of foll 2 rows.
Leave rem 37[41] sts on a holder for centre back neck.

Left front

With No 10/3¼mm needles cast on 62[74] sts. Work 20 rows twisted rib as given for back, inc one st at end of last row. 63[75] sts.
Change to No 8/4mm needles.
Work in patt as given for back until front measures same as back to armhole marker.
Mark each end of next row with contrast coloured threads to denote beg of armhole.
Cont without shaping until front measures 10 rows less than back to shoulder, (approx 60 more patt rows), thus ending with a 2nd or 12th row.

Shape neck

1st row Patt to last 16 sts, sl these sts on to holder.
2nd row P2 tog, patt to end.
3rd row Patt to last 2 sts, K2 tog.
Rep 2nd and 3rd rows once more. 43[53] sts.
Work 5 rows without shaping, thus ending with a 12th or 2nd row.

Shape shoulder

Keeping patt correct throughout, cast off 11[13] sts at beg of next and foll 2 alt rows. Work one row.
Cast off rem 10[14] sts.

Right front

Work to match left front reversing neck and shoulder shaping and working neck edge decs as sl 1, K1, psso on Rs rows and P2 tog tbl on Ws rows.

Sleeves

With No 10/3¼mm needles cast on 62 sts for both sizes and work 20 rows twisted rib as given for back, inc one st at end of last row. 63 sts.
Change to No 8/4mm needles and work in patt as given for back, inc one st at each end of 5th and every foll 5th row until there are 99 sts, working extra sts into patt when possible.
Cont without shaping until sleeve measures 15½[17]in/39.5[43] cm from beg, ending with a 10th or 20th patt row.
Cast off loosely.

Neckband

Join shoulder seams.
With Rs of work facing and No 10/3¼mm needles, K across 16 sts from right front neck holder, pick up and K7 sts up right side of neck shaping, K across 37[41] sts from back neck holder, pick up and K8 sts down left side of neck shaping and K across 16 sts from left front neck holder. 84[88] sts.
Work 13 rows twisted rib as given for back.
Cast off loosely in rib.

Buttonhole band

With Rs of work facing and No 10/3¼mm needles, pick up and K170[180] sts evenly along right front edge to top of neckband.
Work 3 rows twisted rib as given for back.
Next row (buttonhole row) Rib 3[4] sts, *K2 tog, yfwd, rib 16[17] sts, rep from * to last 5 sts, K2 tog, yfwd, rib 3 sts to end.
Work 5 more rows twisted rib.
Cast off in rib.

Button band

Work as given for buttonhole band, beg at top of neckband to pick up sts down left front and omitting buttonholes.

To make up

Press as directed on ball band, omitting ribbing.
Join cast off edge of sleeves to armhole edges of back and front between markers.
Join side and sleeve seams.
Sew on buttons to correspond with buttonholes.

Opposite: The timeless beauty of candlelight pattern enhances this useful button-to-neck cardigan. It is worked in a Shetland Double Knitting yarn and has a dropped shoulder-line.
Designed by Betty Barnden.

Shetland lace shawl

This delicate lace shawl could become your own family heirloom of the future. It is worked in an authentic Shetland lace wool, which is as lightweight as thistledown.

The centre of the shawl features scattered cable twists, which add texture to the fabric but, if you prefer, it could be worked in garter stitch. The scalloped border is worked in Old Shale pattern and the pointed lace edging also repeats the cable theme.

Measurement

60 × 60in/153 × 153cm square

Materials

8 × 1 oz/ or 9 × 25g balls of Jamieson's Shetland lace 2 ply
One pair No 6/5mm needles
Cable needle
The quantity given is based on average requirements and is approximate

Tension

20 sts and 24 rows to 4in/10cm over st st when unstretched worked on No 6/5mm needles

Shawl centre

With No 6/5mm needles cast on 2 sts and begin at one corner. Work in cable patt as folls, or inc on every row as given and work in g st throughout.
1st row (Ws) Loop the yarn right round the right hand needle to inc one — abbreviated as yrn —, P2, turn.
2nd row Yrn, K3, turn.
3rd row Yrn, K1, P2, K1, turn.
4th row Yrn, K5, turn.
5th row Yrn, K1, P4, K1, turn.
6th row Yrn, K7, turn.
7th row Yrn, K1, P6, K1, turn.
8th row Yrn, K9, turn.
9th row Yrn, K1, P8, K1, turn.
10th row Yrn, K11, turn.
11th row Yrn, K1, P10, K1, turn.
12th row Yrn, K4, sl next 3 sts on to cable needle and hold at front of work, K3 from left hand needle

then K3 from cable needle — abbreviated as C6F —, K3, turn.
13th row Yrn, K1, P12, K1, turn.
14th row Yrn, K15, turn.
15th row Yrn, K1, P14, K1, turn.
16th row Yrn, K17, turn.
17th row Yrn, K1, P16, K1, turn.
18th row Yrn, K19, turn.
19th row Yrn, K1, P18, K1, turn.
20th row Yrn, K21, turn.
21st row Yrn, K1, P20, K1, turn.
22nd row Yrn, K23, turn.
23rd row Yrn, K1, P22, K1, turn. 25 sts, including yrn on needle.
Next row Yrn, K4, C6F, K6, C6F, K3.
Cont in patt as now set, making one st at the beg of every row, working 11 rows in st st and on every 12th row working a cable row as foll:
Cable row Yrn, K4, *C6F, K6, rep from * until 9 sts rem, C6F, K3.
Cont until there are 121 sts on needle, ending with a P row.
Next row Yrn, K1, K2 tog tbl, K1, *C6F, K6, rep from * until 9 sts rem, C6F, K2 tog, K1.
Next row Yrn, K2 tog, P to last 3 sts, P2 tog, K1.
Next row Yrn, K1, K2 tog tbl, K to last 3 sts, K2 tog, K1.
Cont dec in this way, making a cable row on every 12th row as foll:
Cable row Yrn, K1, K2 tog tbl, K1, *C6F, K6, rep from * until 9 sts rem, C6F, K2 tog, K1.
Cont until 6 sts rem on needle.
Next row Yrn, K1, (P2 tog) twice, K1.
Next row Yrn, K1, K3 tog, K1.
Next row Yrn, K1, P3 tog.
Next row K3 tog. Fasten off.

First side of border

With Rs of work facing and No 6/5mm needles, beg at the starting point of shawl centre and pick up and K60 sts through the loops on the edge, up to the next corner of the centre.
Next row *K1, K twice into next st, rep from * to end of row. 90 sts.
1st row (Rs) Yrn, (K2 tog) 3 times, *(yfwd, K1) 6 times, (K2 tog) 6 times, rep from * to last 12 sts, (yfwd, K1) 6 times, (K2 tog) 3 times.

Working yrn at beg of every row, work 3 rows g st, noting that these 3 rows are rep between every patt row.
5th row Yrn, K2, (K2 tog) 3 times, *(yfwd, K1) 6 times, (K2 tog) 6 times, rep from * until 14 sts rem, (yfwd, K1) 6 times, (K2 tog) 3 times, K2. 95 sts.
9th row Yrn, K4, yfwd, (K2 tog) 3 times, *(yfwd, K1) 6 times, (K2 tog) 6 times, rep from * until 16 sts rem, (yfwd, K1) 6 times, (K2 tog) 3 times, yfwd, K4. 101 sts.
13th row Yrn, K3, (yfwd, K1) twice, (K2 tog) 4 times, *(yfwd, K1) 6 times, (K2 tog) 6 times, rep from * until 19 sts rem, (yfwd, K1) 6 times, (K2 tog) 4 times, (K1, yfwd) twice, K3. 107 sts.
17th row Yrn, K3, (yfwd, K1) 3 times, (K2 tog) 5 times, *(yfwd, K1) 6 times, (K2 tog) 6 times, rep from * until 22 sts rem, (yfwd, K1) 6 times, (K2 tog) 5 times, (yfwd, K1) 3 times, K3. 113 sts.
21st row Yrn, K3, (yfwd, K1) 4 times, *(K2 tog) 6 times, (yfwd, K1) 6 times, rep from * until 19 sts rem, (K2 tog) 6 times, (yfwd, K1) 4 times, K3. 119 sts.
25th row Yrn, K3, K2 tog, (yfwd, K1) 5 times, *(K2 tog) 6 times, (yfwd, K1) 6 times, rep from * until 22 sts rem, (K2 tog) 6 times, (yfwd, K1) 5 times, K2 tog, K3. 125 sts.
29th row Yrn, K3, (K2 tog) twice, *(yfwd, K1) 6 times, (K2 tog) 6 times, rep from * until 13 sts rem, (yfwd, K1) 6 times, (K2 tog) twice, K3. 131 sts.
33rd row Yrn, K3, yfwd, K1, (K2 tog) 3 times, *(yfwd, K1) 6 times, (K2 tog) 6 times, rep from * until 16 sts rem, (yfwd, K1) 6 times, (K2 tog) 3 times, K1, yfwd, K3. 137 sts.

Opposite: This superb example of an authentic Shetland lace Christening shawl has been reproduced by kind permission of Peter Jamieson. If you prefer, it can be worked in traditional muted colours, with the centre in miniature cable pattern as shown, or garter stitch, and the borders in stripes.

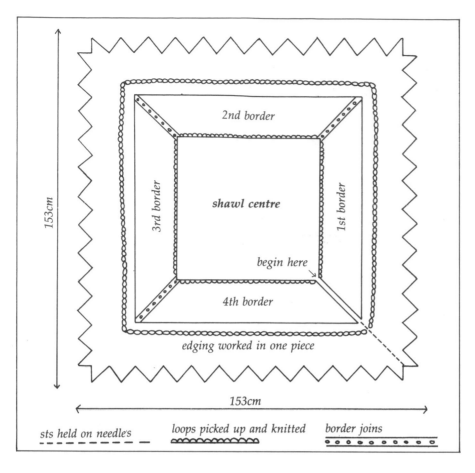

2nd border

3rd border

shawl centre

1st border

begin here

4th border

edging worked in one piece

153cm (left side)

153cm (bottom)

sts held on needles – – – – –

loops picked up and knitted ◠◠◠◠◠◠

border joins ●○●○●○●○●

10th row As 2nd row but K13 instead of K9.

11th row (Yfwd, K2 tog) 4 times, yfwd, K3, (K2 tog, yfwd) twice, C6F, K4, K2 tog, yfwd, K2, K2 tog.

12th row As 2nd row but K14 instead of K9.

13th row (Yfwd, K2 tog) 4 times, yfwd, K4, (K2 tog, yfwd) twice, K10, K2 tog, yfwd, K2, K2 tog.

14th row As 2nd row but K15 instead of K9.

15th row Cast off 6 sts noting that one st rem on right hand needle, K1, K2 tog, yfwd, K2 tog, K1, (K2 tog, yfwd) twice, K3, C6B, K1, K2 tog, yfwd, K2, K2 tog.

16th row Sl 1, K2 tog, yfwd, K1, K2 tog, yfwd, P9, K8, yfwd, K2 tog.

Rep these 16 rows until all the border sts have been used but end on a 15th row.

Leave these 25 sts on holder.

2nd, 3rd and 4th borders and edging

With the Rs of work facing and No 6/5mm needles, pick up and K60 through the loops on the edge of the next side of the shawl centre.

Rep the 60 border patt row.

Transfer the 25 sts from the holder of the previous edging and work them as the 16th row of edging. Cont working the edging as from 1st row until this side has been completed.

Knit the 3rd and 4th sides in the same way.

When the 15th row of last edging has been worked, pick up the 25 sts originally cast on for the edging and graft these tog with the 25 sts on needle.

To make up

Sew tog loops from corresponding sides of border with a fine herringbone stitch.

Damp shawl thoroughly and pin out all the points and leave to dry away from direct heat.

37th row Yrn, K3, (yfwd, K1) twice, (K2 tog) 4 times, *(yfwd, K1) 6 times, (K2 tog) 6 times, rep from * until 19 sts rem, (yfwd, K1) 6 times, (K2 tog) 4 times, (yfwd, K1) twice, K3. 143 sts.

41st row As 17th row. 149 sts.

45th row As 21st row. 155 sts.

49th row As 25th row. 161 sts.

53rd row As 29th row. 167 sts.

57th row As 33rd row. 173 sts.

Working a loop at beg of each row, work 3 rows g st. 176 sts.

Edging

With 176 sts of border on needle, cast on a further 25 sts, turn.

1st row Across 25 cast on sts work (yfwd, K2) 5 times, yfwd, K10, K2 tog, yfwd, K2, taking one from cast on sts and one from border sts K2 tog. (Take one from border sts in this way on every alt row.)

2nd row Sl 1, K2 tog, yfwd, K1, K2 tog, yrn, P9, K9, yfwd, K2 tog.

3rd row (Yfwd, K2 tog) 3 times, yfwd, K1, (K2 tog, yfwd) twice, C6F, K4, K2 tog, yfwd, K2, K2 tog.

4th row As 2nd row but K10 instead of K9.

5th row (Yfwd, K2 tog) 6 times, yfwd, K10, K2 tog, yfwd, K2, K2 tog.

6th row As 2nd row but K11 instead of K9.

7th row (Yfwd, K2 tog) 4 times, yfwd, K1, (K2 tog, yfwd) twice, K3, sl next 3 sts on to cable needle and hold at back of work, K3 from left hand needle then K3 from cable needle — abbreviated as C6B —, K1, K2 tog, yfwd, K2, K2 tog.

8th row As 2nd row but K12 instead of K9.

9th row (Yfwd, K2 tog) 4 times, yfwd, K2, (K2 tog, yfwd) twice, K10, K2 tog, yfwd, K2, K2 tog.

Fair Isle knitting

*As shown in this old photograph, traditional Fair Isle patterns
have not changed much over the years.
The garments worn by this venerable inhabitant of the Island
would have been practical and weatherproof, as well as colourful,
to offer protection against inclement weather.*

Fair Isle knitting

Situated far to the north of Britain and some two hundred miles off the coast of Norway, lie the Shetland Isles. Although the whole group consists of more than one hundred islands, only a few of them are inhabited but their remoteness and the surrounding tumultuous seas have never been a barrier to trade and commerce.

These islands are the acknowledged home of multi-coloured knitting and they have played an important part in perfecting a technique derived from many different sources. In the ninth and tenth centuries immigrants from Norway settled in Shetland, bringing with them their knitting traditions, and these had an influence on the type of coloured knitting developed in the islands. Because of easy access to so many outside influences, however, it is almost impossible to trace the original source of authentic Shetland patterns.

The small island known as Fair Isle lies south of the main Shetland group, off the northern coast of Scotland. It gives its name to a unique type of coloured knitting, which is believed to be Spanish in origin. It has been accepted into local folklore and, indeed, encouraged, that about the time William Lee was perfecting his knitting frame, one of the ships of the Spanish Armada was wrecked off the coast of Fair Isle. Legend has it that the inhabitants of the island were quick to master the techniques of Spanish coloured knitting, either being taught by the sailors who survived the wreck, or by copying the patterns on the garments of dead sailors washed ashore. Some of the traditional stitch patterns bear such names as 'The Armada Cross', 'The Star of Bethlehem' and 'The Crown of Glory', which have Catholic connotations and would not seem to be representative of the normal way of life in the islands, so perhaps there is some truth in this romantic story. On the other hand, such names could originally have been a deliberate ploy to promote the legend!

No examples of Fair Isle knitting as we know it today can be traced before the middle of the nineteenth century. The main knitting industry in Shetland until that time depended upon hand-knitted woollen stockings and the production of fine lace. With the introduction of the industrial revolution, however, the demand for stockings and lace declined but the popularity of coloured knitting increased and Fair Isle caps, scarves, gloves and purses were very much in demand in Victorian times. By the end of the nineteenth century, multi-coloured sweaters began to appear, similar in shape to fishermens' ganseys. These were lifted into the realm of high fashion early in the twentieth century when the Prince of Wales, later to become Edward VIII,

wore the one presented to him by the Fair Isle knitters to play golf on the St. Andrews course. Sweaters and pullovers, worn with plus fours, became the instant vogue.

In common with fishermens' ganseys and guernseys, Fair Isle garments were practical and wind and weather-proof. Using two strands of wool at a time produces a fabric of double thickness. The Fair Isle knitters worked all their garments in the round on sets of needles. This method is particularly useful when working coloured patterns, as the right side of the work is always facing you so every round is knitted. When working in small motifs, each one would have a different background colour and on the larger motifs, two background colours would often be introduced. Where the knitting had to be divided, such as at the armholes, the work was continued in rows, keeping the colour sequence correct throughout by breaking off the wool at the end of each row and rejoining it at the beginning of the next. Fair Isle knitters prided themselves on never repeating the same pattern twice, or the same colour combination more than once on a garment. No more than two colours at a time would be used in any row and the number of stitches worked in a colour were never so great that the yarn could not comfortably be stranded across the back of the fabric until it was required again to work the next set of stitches in that colour. Although many of the patterns needed large multiples of stitches to complete them, these were offset by small seeding patterns and motif designs, which were extensively used in a garment.

As with all knitting, the lines of demarcation between one tradition and another have slowly been eroded and today we tend to think of all multi-coloured knitting as Fair Isle designs. Instead of knitting in rounds, we prefer to work each separate section of a garment in rows throughout, seaming them together when the knitting is completed. Because of the tedium of changing the yarn at the beginning of every row in the authentic colour sequence, it has become common practice to work Fair Isle patterns over two, or more rows of the same colour. Small patterns have become more popular than the complexities of some of the larger patterns but there is nothing to stop the avid knitter from working just one band of a large pattern above the welt and cuffs of a plain sweater.

This section continues with information about Fair Isle techniques and features step-by-step instructions for working some of the traditional patterns. The designs which follow are up-to-date examples of this lovely craft, worked in luxurious or modern, easy-care yarns.

Fair Isle knitting

The technique for working coloured knitting is relatively easy to master, providing you bear two important factors in mind. The first is to keep the knitting tension correct; if you pull the yarn across the back of the work from one set of stitches to another too tightly, the fabric will pucker. The method of weaving in the yarn explained in this section will overcome this problem.

The other point to remember is the exact place you have reached in a pattern row and to keep the colour sequence correct. If you have difficulty in reading from a Fair Isle chart, it is worthwhile taking the time to write out each row before you begin to knit.

Reading from a chart

The instructions for Fair Isle patterns are very long and to save space in a magazine or book, they are reproduced in chart form. Each square on the graph represents one stitch horizontally across the chart, and one row of squares shows the pattern vertically from the lower edge to the top of the chart.

The chart shows the multiples of stitches required for each repeat of the pattern, plus any additional edge stitches which are needed to ensure that the pattern matches correctly at the side seams.

Each colour used in a design is coded with a different letter in the instructions, the main colour as 'A', the first contrast as 'B', the second contrast as 'C', and so on. These letters are then represented by different symbols on the chart.

Working in rows

Unless otherwise stated in the instructions, the odd numbered rows shown on the chart are knitted to form the right side of the fabric, and the even numbered rows are purled for the wrong side of the work.

Begin the first row at the lower right hand corner of the chart, and knit across the row. Repeat the multiples of stitches shown and work any edge stitches at the beginning and end of the row only. Begin the second row at the lower left hand corner of the chart, and purl across the row, working the edge stitches as before.

Continue in this way, working from right to left on the knit rows and from left to right on the purl rows.

Working in rounds

As the right side of the work is always facing you with this method, all the rounds are knitted and the body of the garment is seamless.

Begin the first round at the lower right hand corner of the chart and work across to the left hand corner. Only work the multiples of stitches required for each pattern repeat, omitting any edge stitches shown on the chart. Begin the second round at the right hand side of the chart again and work across to the left hand side, then continue in this way for the length required.

When the work has to be divided, continue as given for working in rows.

Helping hand

Fair Isle knitting is easier to control if you hold one colour in your right hand and the other colour in your left hand, weaving the yarn in across the back of the fabric as each row, or round, is worked.

To weave in the yarn on a knit row, keep both yarns at the back of the work throughout. Each time a new colour is introduced, knit the first stitch with the first colour held in the right hand. On the second and every following alternate stitch in the first colour, put the point of the right hand needle through the stitch from the front to the back, use the left hand to take the contrast colour not in use over the top of the right hand needle from right to left, then knit the stitch with the first colour in the usual way. Knit the third and every following alternate stitch in the usual way without weaving in the contrast yarn, (see Fig 1).

To weave in the yarn on a purl row, keep both yarns at the front of the work throughout. Each time a new colour is introduced, purl the first *two* stitches with the first colour held in the right hand, noting that this will alter the position of the woven stitches. On the third and every following alternate stitch in the first colour, put the point of the right hand needle through the stitch from right to left, use the left hand to take the contrast colour not in use over the top of the right hand needle from right to left, then purl the stitch with the first colour in the usual way. Purl the fourth and every following alternate stitch in the usual way without weaving in the contrast yarn, (see Fig 2).

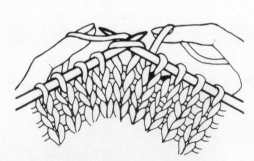

fig 1 weaving in yarn on a knit row

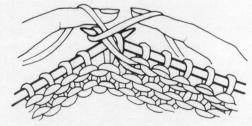

fig 2 weaving in yarn on a purl row

Traditional Fair Isle patterns

These patterns were originally worked in fine hand-spun and hand-dyed wool, but they look just as effective in modern, easy-care double knitting yarns.

Diamond motif

An old traditional pattern which looks most effective and is very simple to knit. This example is worked over multiples of 6 stitches, plus 1, eg 37.

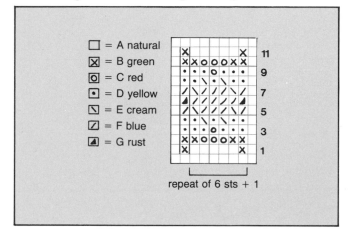

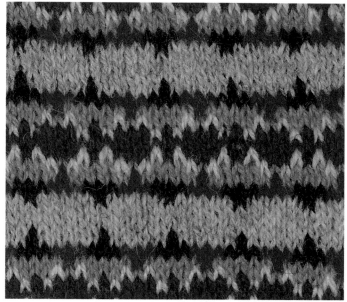

Zigzag motif

This simple pattern forms a very bold motif. This example uses the same background and design colour for most of the rows to avoid too many changes of yarn, and is worked over multiples of 6 stitches, plus 1, eg 37.

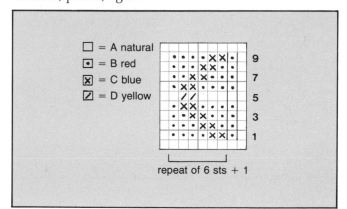

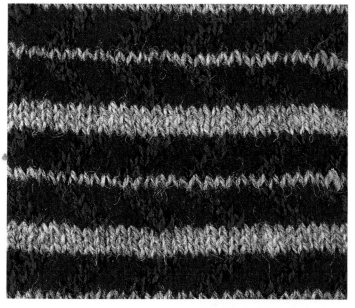

Oxox motif

A delightful design which is very old and is based on a sequence of O's and X's, hence its name. It is one of the most popular of the smaller designs and this example is worked over multiples of 12 stitches, plus 1, eg 37.

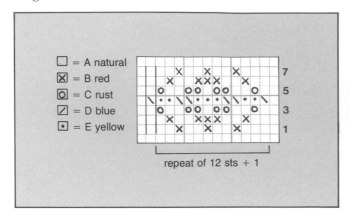

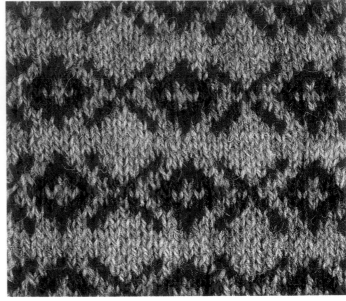

Heart motif

An old and romantic pattern which is very popular. This example is worked over multiples of 12 stitches, plus 1, eg 37.

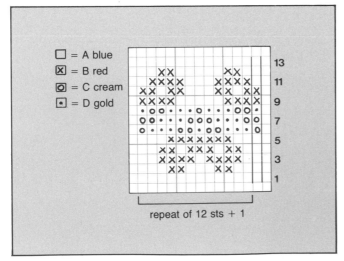

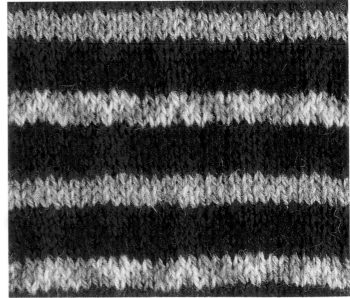

Star motif

There are many different versions of this design but they are all extremely colourful and form large, repeating patterns. This example is worked over multiples of 24 stitches, plus 1, eg 49.

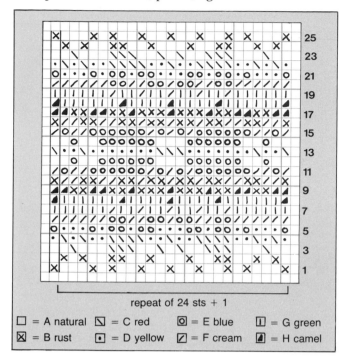

repeat of 24 sts + 1

☐ = A natural   ◣ = C red   ⊙ = E blue   ▯ = G green
☒ = B rust   ⊡ = D yellow   ◪ = F cream   ◢ = H camel

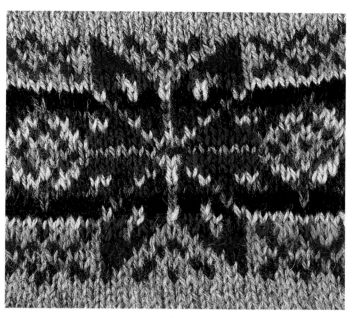

Flower motif

Another large motif which has many different variations, used as a repeating pattern. This example is worked over multiples of 24 stitches, plus 1, eg 49.

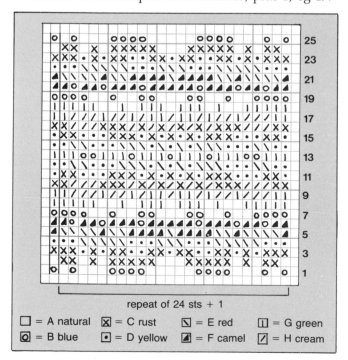

repeat of 24 sts + 1

☐ = A natural   ☒ = C rust   ◣ = E red   ▯ = G green
⊙ = B blue   ⊡ = D yellow   ◪ = F camel   ◪ = H cream

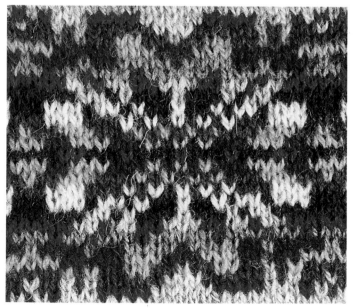

Fair Isle slipover

This V-necked slipover is made in a very wide size range and can be knitted in Merino or Alpaca qualities.
Four different bands of Fair Isle patterns are repeated throughout and five colours are used.

Measurements

To fit 36[38:40:42:44:46]in/ 91[97:102:107:112:117]cm bust/ chest
Actual measurements, 42[44½:47:49½:52:54½]in/ 107[113:119:126:132:138]cm
Length to shoulder, 24½[25:25:25½:26:26½]in/ 62[63:63:65:66:67]cm
The figures in [] refer to the 38/97, 40/102, 42/107, 44/112 and 46in/ 117cm sizes respectively

Materials

3[3:3:3:4:4] × 50g balls of Jaeger Matchmaker Merino 4 ply *or* Jaeger Alpaca knits as 4 ply in main shade A
2[2:2:2:3:3] balls of same in contrast colour B
2[2:2:2:3:3] balls of same in contrast colour C
2[2:2:2:3:3] balls of same in contrast colour D

1[1:1:1:2:2] balls of same in contrast colour E
One pair No 12/2¾mm needles (No 13/2¼mm for Alpaca)
One pair No 10/3¼mm needles (No 11/3mm for Alpaca)
The quantities of yarn given are based on average requirements and are approximate

Tension

32 sts and 32 rows to 4in/10cm over Fair Isle patt and 28 sts and 36 rows over st st, worked on No 10/3¼mm needles and Merino and No 11/3mm needles and Alpaca

Note

When working in patt from charts, strand yarn not in use loosely across back of work over not more than 3 sts at a time to keep fabric elastic. When working from charts A and C read odd rows as K from right to left and even rows as P from left to right. When working from charts B and D, read odd rows as P from left to right and even rows as K from right to left

Back

**With No 12/2¾mm for Merino, or No 13/2¼mm needles for Alpaca and A, cast on 125[133:141:149:155:163] sts.
1st row (Rs) K1, *P1, K1, rep from * to end.
2nd row P1, *K1, P1, rep from * to end.
Rep these 2 rows until work measures 2¾in/7cm from beg, ending with a 1st row.
Next row (inc row) Rib 6[8:9:11:9:10] sts, *M1 by picking up loop lying between needles and K tbl, rib 2, M1, rib 3, rep from * to last 4[5:7:8:6:8] sts, rib to end. 171[181:191:201:211:221] sts.
Change to No 10/3¼mm for Merino, or No 11/3mm needles for Alpaca and joining in and breaking off colours as required, work in patt from charts as foll:-
1st to 7th rows In patt from Chart A, rep 6 patt sts 28[30:31:33:35:36] times across the rows, working first 2[1:3:2:1:3] sts and last

Opposite: This V-necked slipover features four simple Fair Isle patterns worked in bands throughout the design. Designed by Debbie Jenkins.

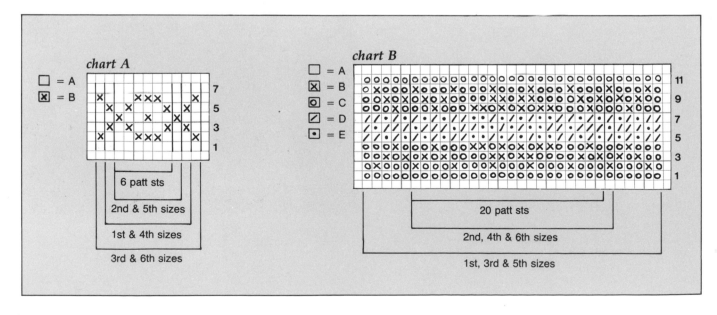

1[0:2:1:0:2] sts on K rows and first 1[0:2:1:0:2] sts and last 2[1:3:2:1:3] sts on P rows as indicated.

8th to 18th rows In patt from chart B, rep 20 patt sts 8[9:9:10:10:11] times across the rows, working first 5[0:5:0:5:0] sts and last 6[1:6:1:6:1] sts on P rows and first 6[1:6:1:6:1] sts and last 5[0:5:0:5:0] sts on K rows as indicated.

19th to 25th rows In patt from chart C, rep 6 patt sts 28[30:31:33:35:36] times across the rows, working first 2[1:3:2:1:3] sts and last 1[0:2:1:0:2] sts on K rows and first 1[0:2:1:0:2] sts and last 2[1:3:2:1:3] sts on P rows as indicated.

26th to 36th rows In patt from chart D, rep 20 patt sts 8[9:9:10:10:11] times across the rows, working first 5[0:5:0:5:0] and last 6[1:6:1:6:1] sts on P rows and first 6[1:6:1:6:1] sts and last 5[0:5:0:5:0] sts on K rows as indicated.

These 36 rows form the patt.
Cont in patt without shaping until work measures 14¼in/36cm from beg, ending with a Ws row.

Shape armholes

Keeping patt correct throughout, cast off 5 sts at beg of next 2 rows.
**

Dec one st at each end of every row until 131[137:143:149:155:157] sts rem, then on every foll alt row until 121[125:131:135:141:145] sts rem.
Cont without shaping until back measures

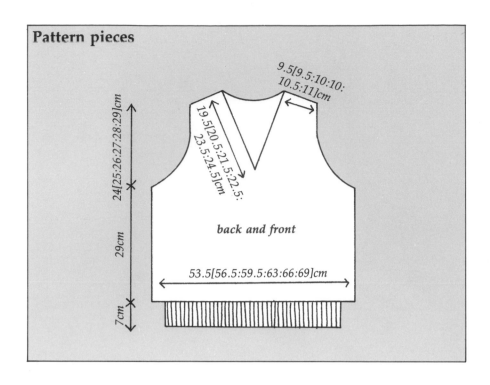

Pattern pieces

9.5[9.5:10:10: 10.5:11]cm

19.5[20.5:21.5:22.5: 23.5:24.5]cm

24[25:26:27:28:29]cm

29cm

back and front

53.5[56.5:59.5:63:66:69]cm

7cm

22¾[23¼:23½:24:24½:24¾]in/ 58[59:60:61:62:63]cm from beg, ending with a Ws row.

Divide for back neck

Next row Patt 37[38:40:41:43:44] sts, turn and leave rem sts on a spare needle.
Dec one st at neck edge on next 8 rows. 29[30:32:33:35:36] sts. Work 5 rows without shaping, ending with a Ws row.

Shape shoulder

Cast off 15[15:16:17:18:18] sts at beg of next row. Work one row. Cast off rem 14[15:16:16:17:18] sts.

With Rs of work facing, sl first 47[49:51:53:55:57] sts from spare needle on to a holder for centre back neck, join appropriate colour to next st and patt to end. Complete left shoulder to match right shoulder, reversing shapings and noting that an extra row must be worked before shoulder shaping.

Front

Work as given for back from ** to **. Dec one st at each end of next 6 rows. 149[159:169:179:189:199] sts.

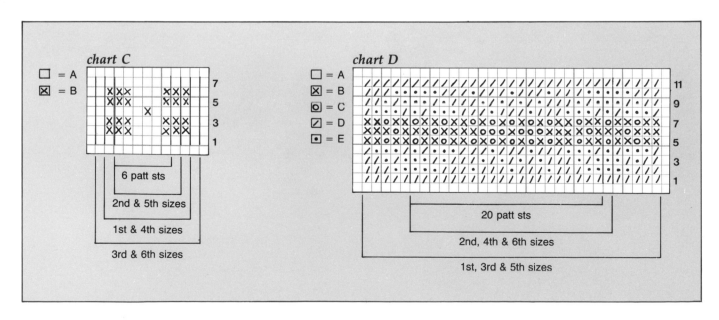

chart C

□ = A
☒ = B

7
5
3
1

6 patt sts

2nd & 5th sizes

1st & 4th sizes

3rd & 6th sizes

chart D

□ = A
☒ = B
⊙ = C
▨ = D
⊡ = E

11
9
7
5
3
1

20 patt sts

2nd, 4th & 6th sizes

1st, 3rd & 5th sizes

Divide for V neck

Next row K2 tog, patt 72[77:82:87:92:97] sts, turn and leave rem sts on a spare needle. Complete left shoulder first.
Next row Patt to last 2 sts, P2 tog. Cont dec one st at armhole edge on every row, *at the same time* dec one st at neck edge on next and every foll alt row until 61[63:65:67:69:68] sts rem.
Now dec one st at each end of every foll alt row until 51[51:53:53:55:56] sts rem. Work one row.
Dec one st at neck edge *only* on next and every foll alt row until 29[30:32:33:35:36] sts rem.
Work without shaping until front measures same as back to shoulder, ending with same patt row as back.

Shape shoulder

Cast off 15[15:16:17:18:18] sts at beg of next row. Work one row.
Cast off rem 14[15:16:16:17:18] sts.
With Rs of work facing, sl centre st on spare needle on to a safety pin, join appropriate colour to next st, patt to last 2 sts, K2 tog.
Complete right shoulder to match left shoulder, reversing shapings and noting that an extra row must be worked before shoulder shaping.

Neck border

Join right shoulder seam.
With Rs of work facing, same needles used for back ribbing and A, pick up and K70[72:74:76:80:84] sts down left side of front neck, K st from safety pin and mark this with coloured thread to denote centre st, pick up and K70[72:74:76:80:84] sts up right side of front neck, 12 sts down right side of back neck, K across 47[49:51:53:55:57] back neck sts on holder dec 7 sts evenly, pick up and K12 sts up left side of back neck. 205[211:217:223:233:243] sts.
1st row (Ws) *P1, K1, rep from * to

within 2 sts of marked centre st, P2 tog, P1, P2 tog tbl, **K1, P1, rep from ** to end.
2nd row K1, *P1, K1, rep from * to within 2 sts of marked centre st, P2 tog, K1, P2 tog tbl, K1, **P1, K1, rep from ** to end.
Rep these 2 rows 3 times more, then 1st row once more.
Cast off loosely in rib, dec each side of centre marked st as before.

Armhole borders

Join left shoulder and neck border seam.

With Rs of work facing, same needles used for back ribbing and A, pick up and K153[155:161:165:173:179] sts evenly round armhole.
Beg with a 2nd row, work in rib as given for back for 9 rows.
Cast off evenly in rib. Work other armhole border in same way.

To make up

Press as directed on ball band, omitting ribbing.
Join side and armhole border seams.

Fair Isle cardigan

This neat, V-necked cardigan is suitable for a man or a woman and is given in a very wide size range. Our colour scheme has been chosen for a woman but it would look most effective in more traditional colours for a man. The button and buttonhole bands are reversible.

Measurements

To fit 32[34:36:38:40:42:44]in/ 81[86:91:97:102:107:112]cm bust/ chest
Actual measurements, 35[37:39:41:43:45:47]in/ 89[94:99:104:109:114:119]cm
Length to shoulder, 22½[23:23:25:25½:26:26½]in/ 57[58:59:63:65:66:67]cm
Sleeve seam, 17[17:17½:18½:18½:18½:19]in/ 43[43:44:47:47:47:48]cm
The figures in [] refer to the 34/86, 36/91, 38/97, 40/102, 42/107 and 44in/112cm sizes respectively

Materials

6[6:6:7:7:8:8:] × 50g balls of Jaeger Alpaca knits as 4 ply in main shade A
2[2:2:2:2:2:2] balls of same in contrast colour B
2[2:2:2:2:2:2] balls of same in contrast colour C
1[2:2:2:2:2:2] balls of same in contrast colour D
One pair No 13/2¼mm needles
One pair No 11/3mm needles
7 buttons
The quantities of yarn given are based on average requirements and are approximate

Tension

32 sts and 32 rows to 4in/10cm over Fair Isle patt worked on No 11/3mm needles

Note

When working in patt from chart, strand yarn not in use loosely across back of work. Read odd rows as K from right to left and even rows as P from left to right

Back

With No 13/2¼mm needles and A, cast on 111[119:127:135:141:149:155] sts.
1st row (Rs) K1, *P1, K1, rep from * to end.
2nd row P1, *K1, P1, rep from * to end.
Rep these 2 rows until work measures 2¾in/7cm from beg, ending with a 1st row.
Next row (inc row) Rib 6[10:1:5:3:7:5], *M1 by picking up loop lying between needles and K tbl, rib 4[4:5:5:5:5:5], rep from * to last 5[9:1:5:3:7:5] sts, M1, rib to end. 137[145:153:161:169:177:185] sts.
Change to No 11 / 3mm needles and joining in and breaking off colours as required, work in patt from chart, rep 4 patt sts 34[36:38:40:42:44:46] times across the rows, working first st on K rows and last st on P rows as indicated.
Cont rep 28 patt rows until back measures 13¾[13¾:13¾:14½:14½:14½:14½]in / 35[35:35:37:37:37:37]cm from beg, ending with a 6th[6th:6th:12th:12th:12th:12th] patt row.

Shape armholes

Keeping patt correct throughout, cast off 4 sts at beg of next 2 rows. Dec one st at each end of next 12[16:16:12:12:16:16] rows. 105[105:113:129:137:137:145] sts. Cont without shaping until armholes measure 8¾[9:9½:10¼:11:11½:11¾]in / 22[23:24:26:28:29:30]cm from beg of shaping, ending with a Ws row.

Shape shoulders

Cast off 10[9:10:12:13:13:14] sts at beg of next 4 rows, then 10[10:11:13:14:13:14] sts at beg of next 2 rows. Cast off rem 45[49:51:55:57:59:61] sts.

Left front

With No 13/2¼mm needles and A, cast on 55[59:63:67:71:75:77] sts. Work 2¾in/7cm rib as given for back, ending with a 1st row.
Next row (inc row) Rib

2[4:6:1:3:5:1], *M1 by picking up loop lying between needles and K tbl, rib 4[4:4:5:5:5:5:], rep from * to last 1[3:5:1:3:5:1] sts, M1, rib to end. 69[73:77:81:85:89:93] sts.
Change to No 11/3mm needles and joining in and breaking off colours as required, work in patt from chart, rep 4 patt sts 17[18:19:20:21:22:23] times across the rows, working first st on K rows and last st on P rows as indicated.
Cont rep 28 patt rows until front measures same as back to underarm, ending with a Ws row.

Shape armhole and front neck

Keeping patt correct throughout, cast off 4 sts at beg of next row for armhole, patt to end. Work one row.
Dec one st at armhole edge on next 12[16:16:12:12:16:16] rows, *at the same time* dec one st at front edge on next and every foll alt row until 47[45:49:59:63:61:65] sts rem.

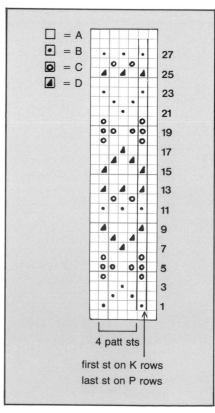

Opposite: This low-buttoning cardigan has been worked in simple Fair Isle patterns and luxurious alpaca yarn. Designed by Debbie Jenkins.

Pattern pieces

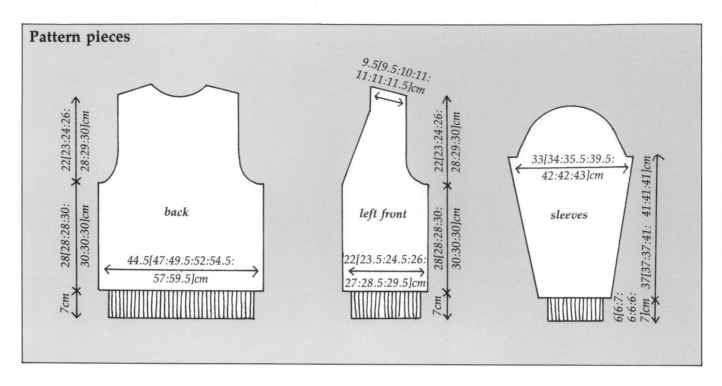

back 22[23:24:26: 28:29:30]cm 28[28:28:30: 30:30:30]cm 7cm 44.5[47:49.5:52:54.5: 57:59.5]cm

left front 9.5[9.5:10:11: 11:11:11.5]cm 22[23:24:26: 28:29:30]cm 28[28:28:30: 30:30:30]cm 7cm 22[23.5:24.5:26: 27:28.5:29.5]cm

sleeves 33[34:35.5:39.5: 42:42:43]cm 37[37:37:41: 41:41:41]cm 6[6:7: 6:6:6: 7]cm

---

Cont dec one st at front edge *only* on next and every foll alt row until 43[41:45:54:58:58:62] sts rem. Cont dec one st at front edge *only* on every foll 3rd row from previous dec until 30[28:31:37:40:39:42] sts rem. Cont without shaping until left front measures same as back to shoulder, ending with a Ws row.

Shape shoulder
Cast off 10[9:10:12:13:13:14] sts at beg of next and foll alt row. Work one row. Cast off rem 10[10:11:13:14:13:14] sts.

Right front
Work as given for left front, reversing all shapings.

Sleeves
With No 13/2¼mm needles and A, cast on 53[53:55:61:61:63:67] sts. Work 2¼[2¼:2¾:2¼:2¼:2¼: 2¾]in/6[6:7:6:6:6:7]cm rib as given for back, ending with a 1st row.
Next row (inc row) Rib 5[4:2:8:8:11:2], *M1 by picking up loop lying between needles and K tbl, rib 4[3:3:3:2:2:3], rep from * to last 4[4:2:8:7:10:2] sts, M1, rib to end. 65[69:73:77:85:85:89] sts. Change to No 11/3mm needles and joining and breaking off colours as required, work in patt from chart, beg with a

1st[1st:1st:21st:21st:21st:21st] patt row, rep 4 patt sts 16[17:18:19:21:21:22] times across the rows, working first st on K rows and last st on P rows as indicated, *at the same time* shape sides by inc one st at each end of 5th[5th:5th:3rd:3rd:3rd:3rd] row and every foll 5th row until there are 105[109:113:125:133:133:137] sts, working extra sts into patt. Cont without shaping until sleeve measures approximately 17[17:17¼:18½:18½:18½:19]in/ 43[43:44:47:47:47:48]cm from beg, ending with same patt row as back before beg armhole shaping.

Shape top
Cast off 4 sts at beg of next 2 rows. Dec one st at each end of next and every foll 4th row until 89[93:97:107:113:107:111] sts rem. Work one row. Dec one st at each end of next and every foll alt row until 71[71:75:87:95:99:103] sts rem. Work one row. Dec one st at each end of every row until 27 sts rem. Cast off rem sts.

Button border
Join shoulder seams. With No 13/2¼mm needles and A, cast on 11 sts.
1st row (Rs) K2, *P1, K1, rep from * to last st, K1.

2nd row *K1, P1, rep from * to last st, K1.
Rep these 2 rows until border, when slightly stretched, fits up left front for a woman or right front for a man and round to centre back of neck. Sew in position as you go along. Cast off evenly in rib.

Buttonhole border
Work as given for button border, making 7 buttonholes, first to come ½in/1cm above lower edge and last to come ½in/1cm below beg of front edge shaping, with 5 more evenly spaced between.

Buttonhole for woman
Next row (Rs) Rib 5, cast off 2 sts, rib to end, turn and rib back, casting on 2 sts above those cast off in previous row.

Buttonhole for man
Next row (Rs) Rib 4, cast off 2 sts, rib to end, turn and rib back, casting on 2 sts above those cast off in previous row.

To make up
Press as directed on ball band, omitting ribbing.
Join side and sleeve seams. Set in sleeves.
Join button and buttonhole borders at centre back of neck.
Sew on buttons.

Simple Fair Isle slipover

This V-necked slipover design is suitable for a man or a woman and is given in a very wide size range. The all-over Fair Isle patterns are worked over multiples of 4 stitches, so are very simple to knit.

Measurements

To fit 32[34:36:38:40:42:44]in/ 81[86:91:97:102:107:112]cm bust/ chest
Actual measurements, 34[36:38:40:41½:43½:45½]in/ 86[91:96:101:106:111:116]cm
Length to shoulder, 21½[22:22½:24:25:25:25½]in/ 55[56:57:61:63:64:65]cm
The figures in [] refer to the 34/86, 36/91, 38/97, 40/102, 42/107 and 44in/112cm sizes respectively

Materials

3[3:3:4:4:4:4] × 50g balls of Jaeger Alpaca knits as 4 ply in main shade A
1[1:1:1:1:1:1] ball of same in contrast colour B
1[2:2:2:2:2:2] balls of same in contrast colour C
1[2:2:2:2:2:2] balls of same in contrast colour D
One pair No 13/2¼mm needles
One pair No 11/3mm needles
The quantities of yarn given are based on average requirements and are approximate

Tension

32 sts and 32 rows to 4in/10cm over Fair Isle patt worked on No 11/3mm needles

Note

When working in patt from chart, strand yarn not in use loosely across back of work. Read odd rows as K from right to left and even rows as P from left to right

Back

**With No 13/2¼mm needles and A, cast on 111[119:127:135:141:149:155] sts.

1st row (Rs) K1, *P1, K1, rep from * to end.
2nd row P1, *K1, P1, rep from * to end.
Rep these 2 rows until work measures 2¾in/7cm from beg, ending with a 1st row.
Next row (inc row) Rib 6[10:1:5:3:7:5], *M1 by picking up loop lying between needles and K tbl, rib 4[4:5:5:5:5:5], rep from * to last 5[9:1:5:3:7:5] sts, M1, rib to end. 137[145:153:161:169:177:185] sts.
Change to No 11/3mm needles and joining in and breaking off colours as required, work in patt from chart rep 4 patt sts 34[36:38:40:42:44:46] times across the rows, working first st on K rows and last st on P rows as indicated.
Cont rep 18 patt rows until back measures 13½[13½:13½:14¼: 14¼:14¼:14¼]in/ 34[34:34:36:36:36:36]cm from beg, or required length to underarm less 1in/2.5cm, ending with a Ws row.

Shape armholes

Keeping patt correct throughout, cast off 4 sts at beg of next 2 rows. Dec one st at each end of next 12[16:16:12:12:16:16] rows. 105[105:113:129:137:137:145] sts. **
Cont without shaping until armholes measure 8¼[8¾:9:9¾:10¾:11:11½]in/ 21[22:23:25:27:28:29]cm from beg of shaping, ending with a Ws row.

Shape shoulders

Cast off 10[9:10:12:13:13:14] sts at beg of next 4 rows, then 10[10:11:13:14:13:14] sts at beg of next 2 rows.
Leave rem 45[49:51:55:57:59:61] sts on a spare needle for centre back neck.

Front

Work as given for back from ** to **.
Keeping patt correct, work 4[0:0:4:4:0:0] rows, ending with a Ws row.

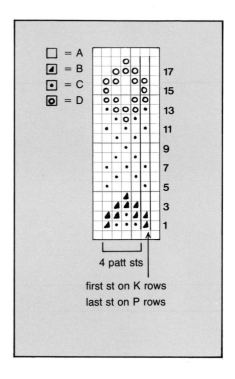

☐ = A
◨ = B
⊡ = C
◉ = D

4 patt sts

first st on K rows
last st on P rows

Divide for V neck

Next row Patt 52[52:56:64:68:68:72] sts, turn and leave rem sts on a spare needle.
Complete left shoulder first.
Work 1[0:0:1:1:1:1] row.

2nd and 3rd sizes only

Dec one st at neck edge *only* on next [3:1] rows.

All sizes

Dec one st at neck edge *only* on next and every foll alt row until 30[28:31:37:40:39:42] sts rem.
Work without shaping until front measures same as back to shoulder, ending with same patt row as back and a Ws row.

Shape shoulder

Cast off 10[9:10:12:13:13:14] sts at beg of next and foll alt row. Work one row. Cast off rem 10[10:11:13:14:13:14] sts.
With Rs of work facing, sl centre st on spare needle on to a safety pin, join appropriate colour to next st, patt to end.
Complete right shoulder to match left shoulder, reversing shapings and noting that an extra row must be worked before shoulder shaping.

Pattern piece

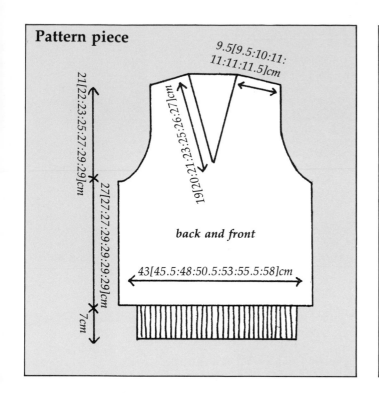

9.5[9.5:10:11:11:11:11.5]cm

19[20:21:23:25:26:27]cm

21[22:23:25:27:29:29]cm

27[27:27:29:29:29:29]cm

7cm

back and front

43[45.5:48:50.5:53:55.5:58]cm

This example shows soft pink and grey, spiced with brown and nutmeg, for a woman's version.

Neck border

Join right shoulder seam.
With Rs of work facing, No 13/2¼mm needles and A, pick up and K51[55:57:63:67:69:71] sts down left side of front neck, K st from safety pin and mark this with coloured thread to denote centre st, pick up and K51[55:57:63:67:69:71] sts up right side of front neck, then K45[49:51:55:57:59:61] sts from back neck holder dec 3 sts evenly. 145[157:163:179:189:195:201] sts.
1st row (Ws) K1, *P1, K1, rep from * to within 2 sts of marked centre st, P2 tog, P1, P2 tog tbl, K1, **P1, K1, rep from ** to end.
2nd row *P1, K1, rep from * to within 2 sts of marked centre st, P2 tog, K1, P2 tog tbl, **K1, P1, rep from ** to end.
Rep these 2 rows 3 times more, then 1st row once more.
With No 11/3mm needle, cast off evenly in rib, dec each side of centre marked st as before.

Armhole borders

Join left shoulder and neck border seam.
With Rs of work facing, No 13/ 2¼mm needles and A, pick up and K117[119:125:131:137:141:145] sts evenly round armhole.
Beg with a 2nd row, work in rib as given for back for 2in/5cm.
With No 11/3mm needle, cast off evenly in rib. Work other armhole border in same way.

To make up

Press as directed on ball band, omitting ribbing.
Join side and armhole border seams.
Fold armhole borders in half to Ws and sl st loosely in position.

Opposite: This simple to knit Fair Isle slipover is suitable for a man or woman and is worked in alpaca yarn. Neat ribbing completes the welt, neck and armbands. Designed by Debbie Jenkins.

Jersey with pattern panels

This striking design features vertical panels of Fair Isle pattern on the body and sleeves, instead of the more traditional horizontal bands. A boldly contrasting pattern defines the yoke across the back and front of the body and the top of the sleeves. A third pattern is introduced on the yoke and above the cuffs.

Measurements

To fit 32[34:36:38:40:42:44]in/ 81[86:91:97:102:107:112]cm bust/ chest loosly
Actual measurements, 42[44:46:48:50:52:54]in/ 107[112:117:122:127:132:137]cm
Length to shoulder, 23½[24:24½:25:25½:25¾:26]in/ 60[61:62:63:64:65:66]cm
Sleeve seam, 16½in/41cm
The figures in [] refer to the 34/86, 36/91, 38/97, 40/102, 42/107 and 44in/112cm sizes respectively

Materials

5[6:7:8:9:10:11] × 50g balls of Wendy Shetland Double Knitting in main shade A
3[3:4:4:5:6:6] balls of same in contrast colour B
4[4:5:5:5:6:6] balls of same in contrast colour C
One pair No 10/3¼mm needles
One pair No 8/4mm needles
The quantities of yarn given are based on average requirements and are approximate

Tension

24 sts and 32 rows to 4in/10cm over st st worked on No 8/4mm needles

Back

With No 10/3¼mm needles and B, cast on 100[106:112:118:124:130:136] sts. Work one row K1, P1 rib. Change to A, K one row, then work 15 rows K1, P1 rib.
Next row (Rs) With B, K to end.
Next row (inc row) P11[1:4:7:10:13:3], *P twice into next st, P2[3:3:3:3:3:4], rep from * 25 times more, P to end. 126[132:138:144:150:156:162] sts. Change to No 8/4mm needles and cont in patt, joining in colours as required.
**1st row (Rs) K (1 C, 2 A) to end.
2nd row P (1 A, 3 C, 1 A, 1 C) to end.
3rd row K (2 C, 3 A, 1 C) to end.
4th row As 2nd row.**
These 4 rows form the patt. Cont in patt until work measures 14in/ 36cm from beg, ending with a Ws row. With C, K one row. With B, P one row, inc one st in centre. 127[133:139:145:151:157:163] sts.
Work the 13 rows of patt from chart.
With B, P one row, dec one st in centre. 126[132:138:144:150:156:162] sts.
Cont in yoke patt as foll:
***1st row (Rs) With A, K one row.
2nd row P (3 A, 3 B) to end.

3rd row K (1 B, 1 A, 1 B, 3 A) to end.
4th row As 2nd row.
5th row As 1st row.
6th row P (3 B, 3 A) to end.
7th row K (3 A, 1 B, 1 A, 1 B) to end.
8th row As 6th row.***
These 8 rows form the yoke patt. Rep them until work measures 23½[24:24½:25:25½:25¾:26]in/ 60[61:62:63:64:65:66]cm from beg, ending with a Ws row.

Shape shoulders

Cast of 10[10:11:11:12:12:12] sts at beg of next 4 rows, then 9[10:10:11:11:12:13] sts at beg of next 4 rows.
Leave rem 50[52:54:56:58:60:62] sts on holder.

Opposite: This jersey is given a new look with vertical panels of Fair Isle patterns on the body and sleeves and a boldly contrasting effect on the yoke and sleeve tops.

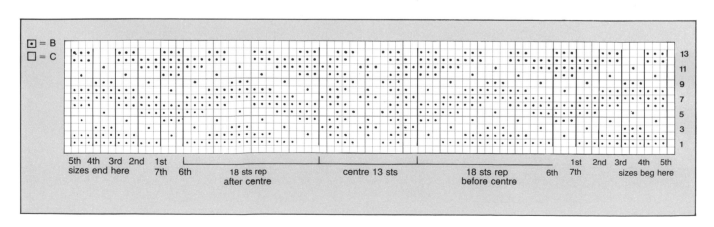

Pattern pieces

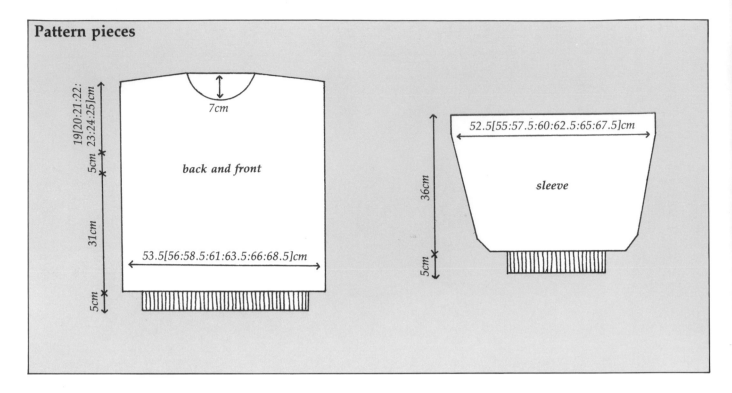

back and front

19[20:21:22:
23:24:25]cm

5cm

31cm

7cm

53.5[56:58.5:61:63.5:66:68.5]cm

5cm

sleeve

52.5[55:57.5:60:62.5:65:67.5]cm

36cm

5cm

Front

Work as given for back to beg of
yoke patt. Work from *** to ***,
then rep the 8 row patt until work
measures 2½in/7cm less than back
to shoulder shaping, ending with
a Ws row.

Shape neck

Next row Patt 55[57:59:61:63:65:67]
sts, turn and cont on these sts only
for first side. On rows beg at *neck
edge*, cast off 3 sts 3 times, 2 sts 3
times, then dec one st at neck edge
on next 2 rows.
38[40:42:44:46:48:50] sts.
Cont without shaping until front
measures same as back to
shoulder, ending at side edge.

Shape shoulder

Cast off 10[10:11:11:12:12:12] sts at
beg of next and foll alt row,
9[10:10:11:11:12:13] sts at beg of
foll 2 alt rows.
With Rs of work facing, sl centre
16[18:20:22:24:26:28] sts on to
holder for front neck, rejoin yarn
to rem sts and patt to end.
Complete this side to match first
side, reversing shaping.

Sleeves

With No 10/3¼mm needles and B,
cast on 54[54:56:58:60:62:64] sts.
Work rib as given for back welt,
inc 12[18:16:14:18:16:14] sts evenly
across the 18th row.
66[72:72:72:78:78:78] sts.
Change to No 8/4mm needles. K
one row C, then P 1 row C.
Rep the 8 patt rows from *** to ***
twice.
Work 2 rows st st with C, inc 12 sts
evenly across last row.
78[84:84:84:90:90:90] sts.
Cont in the 4 row patt from ** to **,
at the same time inc one st at each
end of 3rd row foll and every foll
alt row until there are
126[132:138:144:150:156:162] sts.
Cont without shaping until sleeve
measures 13in/33cm from beg,
ending with a Ws row.
With C, K one row. With B, P one
row inc one st in centre of row.
Work 13 rows of patt from chart.
With B, work 2 rows st st. Cast off
loosely.

Neckband

Join right shoulder seam. With Rs
of work facing, No 10/3¼mm
needles and B, pick up and
K20[21:22:22:23:23:24] sts down
left neck edge, K across
16[18:20:22:24:26:28] sts on holder,
pick up and K20[21:22:22:23:23:24]
sts up right neck edge and
K50[52:54:56:58:60:62] sts on
holder.
106[112:118:122:128:132:138] sts.
With B, work one row K1, P1rib.
Change to A. K one row then
work 2in/5cm K1, P1 rib. Cast off
loosely in rib.

To make up

Press as directed on ball band.
Join left shoulder and neckband.
Fold neckband in half to Ws and sl
st in place.
Fold sleeves in half lengthways
and, placing fold to shoulder
seam, sew cast off edge to back
and front side edges.
Join side and sleeve seams.

Fair Isle jersey with raglan sleeves

These raglan-sleeved jerseys in simple Fair Isle patterns have been designed so that the patterns on the body and at the top of the sleeves form a yoked effect.

Measurements

To fit 34[36:38:40:42]in/ 86[91:97:102:107]cm bust/chest
Actual measurements, 39[41:44:46:48]in/ 99[104:112:117:122]cm
Length to centre back, excluding neckband, 22½[23½:25:25½:26]in/ 57[60:63:65:66]cm
Sleeve seam, 16½[17:18:18:18]in/ 42[43:46:46:46]cm
The figures in [] refer to the 36/91, 38/97, 40/102 and 42in/107cm sizes respectively

Materials

7[7:8:8:8] × 50g balls of Sunbeam pure new wool Double Knitting in main shade A
3[3:4:4:4] balls of same in contrast colour B
2[2:3:3:3] balls of same in contrast colour C
3[3:3:4:4] balls of same in contrast colour D
One pair No 10/3¼mm needles
One pair No 8/4mm needles
Set of four No 10/3¼mm needles pointed at both ends
The quantities of yarn given are based on average requirements and are approximate

Tension

28 sts and 29 rows to 4in/10cm over patt worked on No 8/4mm needles

Front

With No 10/3¼mm needles and A, cast on 107[113:119:125:131] sts.
1st row (Rs) K2, *P1, K1, rep from * to last st, K1.
2nd row K1, *P1, K1, rep from * to end.
Cont in rib as given until work measures 3in/7cm from beg, ending with a Rs row.
Next row (inc row) Rib 9, *inc in next st, rib 2, rep from * to last 8 sts, rib 8. 137[145:153:161:169] sts.
Change to No 8/4mm needles. Beg with a K row cont in patt from chart from rows 1 to 34 in st st, rep the 8 patt sts 17[18:19:20:21] times across and working odd sts as indicated.
Cont in patt for a further 34[38:46:46:46] more rows.

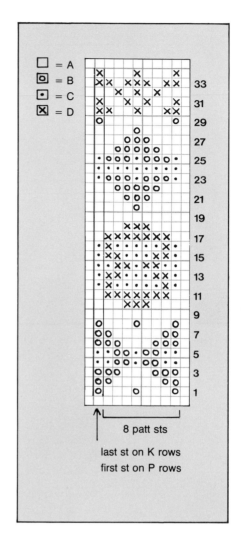

= A
= B
= C
= D

8 patt sts

last st on K rows
first st on P rows

Pattern pieces

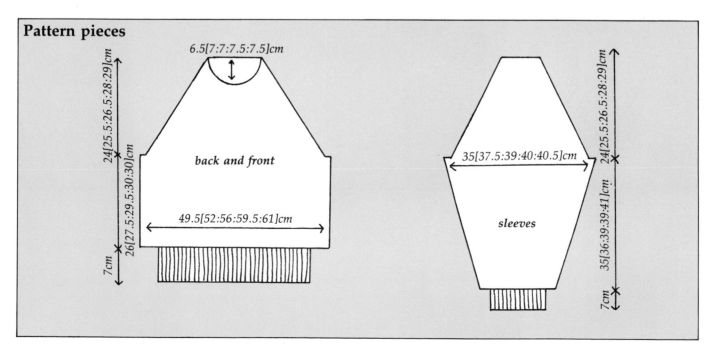

6.5[7:7:7.5:7.5]cm

24[25.5:26.5:28:29]cm

26[27.5:29.5:30:30]cm

7cm

back and front

49.5[52:56:59.5:61]cm

35[37.5:39:40:40.5]cm

24[25.5:26.5:28:29]cm

35[36:39:39:41]cm

7cm

sleeves

Shape raglan armholes

Keep patt correct throughout, cast off 2 sts at beg of next 2 rows, then dec one st at each end of every Rs row until 99[105:111:117:123] sts rem. P 1 row.**

Now dec one st at each end of every row until 67[73:75:81:87] sts rem, thus ending after a P row.

Shape neck

Next row Work 2 tog, patt 21[23:23:25:27] sts, turn.
Complete left side first. Cont dec one st at raglan edge on every row as before, *at the same time* dec one st at neck edge on next 5 rows. 12[14:14:16:18] sts.
Cont dec at raglan edge only until 2 sts rem.
Next row P2 tog and fasten off.
With Rs of work facing, sl first 21[23:25:27:29] sts on to holder and leave for centre front neck, rejoin yarn to rem sts, patt to last 2 sts, K2 tog.
Complete right side as given for left side, reversing shaping.

Back

Work as given for front to **.
Now dec one st at each end of every row until 35[37:39:41:43] sts rem. Sl sts on to a holder and leave for centre back neck.

Sleeves

With No 10/3¼mm needles and A, cast on 43[45:47:49:51] sts. Work in rib as given for front for 3in/7cm, ending with a Rs row.
Next row (inc row) Rib 6[8:6:8:10], inc one in each of next 30[28:34:32:30] sts, rib to end. 73[73:81:81:81] sts.
Change to No 8/4mm needles. Beg with a K row work in st st and patt from chart, beg with 5th[5th:7th:7th:7th] row, *at the same time* shape sleeve by inc one st at each end of the 11th[9th:7th:7th:5th] row foll, then on every foll 6th[4th:6th:6th:4th] row until there are 81[81:93:91:93]

sts, then on every foll 6th [6th:8th:6th:6th] row until there are 101[105:109:113:117] sts, working extra sts into patt.
Work 9[9:7:11:11] rows without shaping, thus ending on same row of patt as on front and back before raglan shaping.

Shape top

Keep patt correct throughout, cast off 2 sts at beg of next 2 rows. Dec one st at each end of every Rs row until 53 sts rem, then on every row until 7 sts rem. Sl sts on to holder.

Neckband

Join raglan seams.
With Rs of work facing, set of four

No 10/3¼mm needles and A, K across 7 sts on left sleeve holder, pick up and K14[16:18:20:22] sts down left front neck, K across sts on front neck holder, K up 14[16:18:20:22] sts up right front neck, K across 7 sts on right sleeve holder and 35[37:39:41:43] on back neck holder. 98[106:114:122:130] sts.
Work 16 rounds K1, P1 rib. Cast off loosely in rib.

To make up

Press as directed on ball band, omitting ribbing.
Join side and sleeve seams. Fold neckband in half to Ws and sl st down. Press seams.

*Opposite: Bands of Fair Isle patterns have been worked on this raglan-sleeved jersey, forming a yoked effect where the shaping takes place.
Designed by Pat Menchini.*

Fair Isle jersey

The basic shape of this design means the minimum of shaping. The size range, dropped shoulder line and double neckband make it suitable for a man or a woman. The bands of Fair Isle patterns are all worked over the same multiples of stitches, so the design is easy to knit. We have chosen bright colours against a cream background but it would look just as effective worked in authentic colours.

Measurements

To fit 34 – 36[38 – 40]in/86 – 91[97 – 102]cm bust/chest
Actual measurements, 41[49]in/ 104[125]cm
Length to shoulder, 25¼[27½]in/ 64[70]cm
Sleeve seam, 17½[19]in/44[48]cm
The figures in [] refer to the 38 – 40in/97 – 102cm size only

Materials

7[8] × 50g balls of Emu Superwash Double Knitting in main shade A
2[3] balls of same in contrast colour B
3[3] balls of same in contrast colour C
2[2] balls of same in contrast colour D
2[2] balls of same in contrast colour E
1[2] balls of same in contrast colour F
One pair No 10/3¼mm needles
One pair No 8/4mm needles
One pair No 7/4½mm needles
The quantities of yarn given are based on average requirements and are approximate

Tension

23 sts and 26 rows to 4in/10cm over patt worked on No 7/4½mm needles

Back

With No 10/3¼mm needles and A, cast on 107[129] sts.
1st row (Rs) K1, *P1, K1, rep from * to end.

2nd row P1, *K1, P1, rep from * to end.
Rep these 2 rows for 2½in/7cm, ending with a 1st row.
Next row (inc row) Rib 12[9], *M1 by picking up loop lying between needles and K tbl, rib 7[8], rep from * to last 11[8] sts, M1, rib to end. 120[144] sts.
Change to No 8/4mm needles. Beg with a K row work 4 rows st st. Commence patt.
When working Fair Isle patt rows use *No 7/4½mm* needles, joining in colours as required and stranding yarn loosely across back of work; when working rows of st st in A between Fair Isle patts, use *No 8/4mm* needles.
1st row (Rs) With No 7/4½mm needles, rep 12 sts from chart 10[12] times.
2nd to 4th rows As 1st row.
5th to 8th rows With No 8/4mm needles and A, work 4 rows st st. Cont working from chart in this way, rep the 52 rows throughout, until the back measures 25[27]in/ 64[70]cm from beg, ending with a Ws row.

Shape shoulders

Keeping patt correct, cast off 13[16] sts at beg of next 4 rows, and 13[17] sts at beg of foll 2 rows. Leave rem 42[46] sts on holder for centre back neck.

Front

Work as given for back until front measures 22[24]in/57[62]cm from beg, ending with a Ws row.

Shape neck

Next row Patt 51[62] sts, turn and leave rem sts on a spare needle. Complete left shoulder first. Keeping patt correct throughout, dec one st at neck edge on every row until 39[49] sts rem. Cont without shaping until front measures same as back to shoulder, ending at side edge.

Shape shoulder

Cast off 13[16] sts at beg of next and foll alt row. Work one row. Cast off rem 13[17] sts.

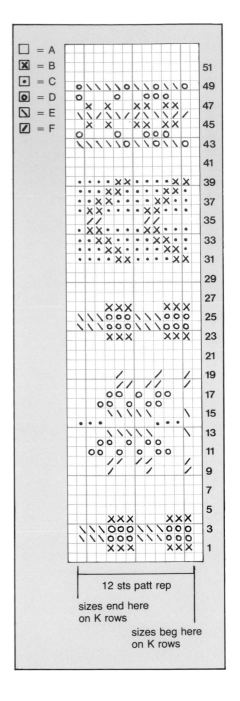

□ = A
☒ = B
⊡ = C
◉ = D
◩ = E
◪ = F

12 sts patt rep

sizes end here on K rows

sizes beg here on K rows

Opposite: This jazzy jersey gives a new look to traditional Fair Isle motifs. It requires the minimum of shaping and is suitable for a man or woman. Designed by Jan Bird.

Pattern pieces

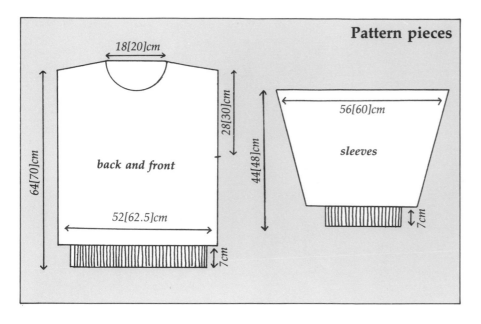

With Rs of work facing, sl first 18[20] sts from spare needle on to a holder for centre front neck, join appropriate colour to next st and patt 51[62] sts.
Complete right shoulder to match left shoulder, reversing shaping.

Sleeves

With No 10/3¼mm needles and A, cast on 49[53] sts. Work 2½in/7cm rib as given for back, ending with a 1st row.
Next row (inc row) Rib 5[9], *M1, rib 4[2], rep from * to last 4[8] sts, M1, rib to end. 60[72] sts.
Change to No 8/4mm needles. Beg with a K row work 4 rows st st. Work in patt from chart as given for back, *at the same time* inc one st at each end of 5th and every foll alt row until there are 124[116] sts, working extra sts into patt, then inc on every foll 4th row from previous inc until there are 128[138] sts, cont to work extra sts into patt.
Cont without shaping until sleeve

measures 17½[19]in/44[48]cm from beg, ending with a Ws row.

Shape top

Cast off 20 sts at beg of next 4 rows.
Cast off rem 48[58] sts.

Neckband

Join right shoulder seam. With Rs of work facing, No 10/3¼mm needles and A, rejoin yarn and pick up and K20[22] sts down left side of front neck, K across front neck sts on holder inc one st at each end, pick up and K20[22] sts up right side of front neck, K across back neck sts on holder inc one st in centre. 103[113] sts.
Beg with a 2nd row, work 2½in/7cm rib as given for back, ending with a 2nd row.
Cast off loosely in rib.

To make up

Press as directed on ball band, omitting ribbing.
Join left shoulder and neckband seam. Fold neckband in half to Ws and sl st down.
Fold sleeves in half lengthways and, placing fold to shoulder seam, sew in sleeves. Join side and sleeve seams.

Icelandic knitting

*This old engraving shows the harsh rugged terrain of an Icelandic farm
and is typical of the country. From earliest records it is
clear that sheep farming was of great importance to the
population and as early as 1581 tenants of the church-owned farms in
Northern Iceland partly paid their rents with knitted stockings.*

Icelandic knitting

Iceland is the second largest island in Europe and the third largest in the Atlantic Ocean, made up of the mainland, which is roughly four-fifths the size of England, and various small islands and skerries. The group lies 261 miles north-west of the Faroe Islands and some 173 miles south-east of the vast region of Greenland, with its extreme northern point touching the Arctic Circle.

The area was settled by the Norwegians during the ninth and tenth centuries but, prior to this, the Irish had discovered the country. Some Irish settlers still remained when the Norwegians arrived but it is not known whether they had already introduced sheep to the region. The Norwegians certainly brought sheep and other farm animals with them, and it is from this original stock that the present sheep of Iceland are descended.

The soils of Iceland contain a low percentage of clay and are very susceptible to erosion. With the arrival of man and grazing livestock, the delicate balance between soil-building and soil-erosion processes was disturbed. Wood cutting, forest fires and a deterioration in the climate devastated the once extensive birch woods and the result was soil destruction on a massive scale. This has always been a handicap and agriculture has been limited in scope and variety, the cultivated areas amounting to about only one per cent of the land mass.

From the earliest written records, it is clear that the husbandry of sheep was of great importance to the population of Iceland. During the fourteenth century, cloth woven from the local wool was one of the main exports of the country but as the demand for this cloth declined, fishing became the main industry. As with all other island communities, the shepherd and fisherman go hand in hand.

In the latter half of the sixteenth century knitting appears to have been introduced to the country and its growth spread rapidly. Many of the newly-arrived Norwegian settlers brought with them a knowledge of their own knitting traditions. Others who came to the country via Scotland, the Shetland Isles and the Faroes, would undoubtedly have exchanged patterns and ideas about the craft with local inhabitants. British and German merchants would also have encouraged the growth of what became an important part of the export trade and remained so for a period of about two hundred years. As early as 1581, the records show that the tenants of church-owned farms in northern Iceland partly paid their rents in kind with knitted stockings.

As with all ancient folk crafts, no preconceived patterns were used and as stitches were invented they were passed from one generation to another by word of mouth. As the craft developed, every design embodied the art and culture of Iceland, drawing inspiration from the stories recorded in the great Sagas, earliest Viking folklore and tales of great kings, bishops and churches.

Although the coloured stitch patterns of Iceland now closely resemble those found in Scandinavia, Shetland and the Faroes, the local wool gives the knitting an instantly recognizable appearance. The original Icelandic sheep belonged to the horned, short-tailed, northern European group, and throughout the centuries it has remained essentially a pure strain, uncrossed with other breeds. Attempts were made in the past to crossbreed and foreign sheep were imported in the eighteenth and nineteenth centuries. On two occasions some Merino sheep were introduced to the country but each time they brought with them the dreaded disease, scab. The imported sheep, their offspring and all the sheep in the neighbouring districts were slaughtered to eradicate the disease.

The fleece of the Icelandic sheep is unique, as it has two different layers of wool; long, coarse outer fibres to protect it from the wind, rain and snow, and finer fibres which grow lower in the fleece, filling in the space between the long fibres. The combination of long guard fibres and short underfleece can be compared to a mixture of mohair and merino. This double coat is found only in Icelandic sheep and allows them to exist comfortably in harsh winters and temperate summers.

Authentic Icelandic wool is not spun in the orthodox way but two threads, one from the inner and one from the outer coat, are lightly twisted together to form a bulky yarn which is very light and hard-wearing. When the wool is knitted into a garment, insulating air is so successfully trapped that the garment is wind and weather-proof. The inner and outer fibres are sorted into distinct shades, varying from creamy-white, through all tones of grey, brown and black. Fashion colours have been introduced but most of the exported wool is in these natural colours, providing another recognizable aspect of traditional Icelandic knitting.

This section continues with methods of knitting in the round, essential for working the yoke of an authentic Icelandic design, followed by two designs worked in pure Icelandic wool.

Knitting in rounds

Traditional Icelandic designs are knitted in stocking stitch in rounds, with a band of coloured pattern above the welt and cuffs, a variation of which is repeated on the circular yoke. The body and sleeves are worked first, but not completed, and the stitches then used to form the yoke, which must be decreased at regular intervals until the size required for the neck opening is obtained. The patterns on the yoke take these decreases into account and rounds in one colour are worked before beginning the next pattern.

Knitting with sets of needles

To produce a seamless, tubular fabric, knitting is worked in rounds with sets of four needles. These come in a range of sizes and each needle is pointed at both ends.

An easy way of casting on with sets of needles is to make the total number of stitches required with two of the needles, and then work one or two *rows* in pattern, as directed in the instructions. Then divide the stitches equally over three of the needles, leaving the fourth to work the stitches, making sure the stitches are not twisted round the needles before continuing to work in rounds. When the garment is completed, thread the cast on end of yarn into a blunt-ended sewing needle and join the gap at the beginning with a few over-sewn stitches.

To knit with sets of needles, use the spare needle to work across the stitches of the first needle of the round; when the first needle is free of stitches, use this to work across the stitches of the second needle, then when the second needle is free, use this to work across the stitches of the third needle. Continue each round in this way.

To cast off with sets of needles, use the free needle to cast off the stitches of the first needle of the round, until one stitch remains on the right hand needle. Put the left hand needle aside. Now use the right hand needle to cast the stitches off the second needle and the third needle, (see Fig 1). Fasten off in the usual way.

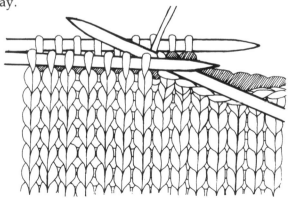

fig 1 *casting off the second and third needles of a set of four*

Knitting with a circular needle

Circular needles comprise two pointed needle ends which are joined together by a thin strip of flexible nylon. They can be used for knitting in rounds or rows.

Use the pointed ends of the needle as a pair to cast on the required number of stitches. Before beginning to knit, make sure the stitches are not twisted round the nylon strip which joins the needle ends, (see Fig 2).

fig 2 *casting on with a circular needle*

To knit with a circular needle in rounds, use the right hand needle point to work across all the stitches, until you come to the beginning of the round again. (To knit in rows, turn the work at the end of a row just as you would when using a pair of needles.) When using a circular needle to knit in rounds it is important to use the correct length, to ensure that the stitches will reach from one point to the other without stretching the fabric, see chart given on page 130.

To cast off with a circular needle, use the right hand needle point to work the stitches and the left hand point to lift them over the stitch and off the needle, just as you would when using a pair of needles. Fasten off in the usual way.

Opposite: The coloured yoke on this traditional Icelandic jersey is worked in rounds on a circular needle but the body and sleeves are worked in rows, see pattern on page 112 Designed by Debbie Scott.

Jersey with round yoke

This traditional Icelandic jersey has a coloured patterned yoke, with patterning above the welt and cuffs.
The design is worked in an authentic Icelandic wool and is suitable for a man or a woman.

Measurements

To fit 34 – 36[38 – 40]in/86 – 91[97 – 102]cm bust/chest
Actual measurements, 41¾[45¾]in/106[116]cm
Length to centre back neck, excluding neckband, 26¾[27½]in/68[70]cm
Sleeve seam, 16½[17¾]in/42[45]cm
The figures in [] refer to the 38 – 40in/97 – 102cm size only

Materials

6[7] × 100g balls of Scotnord Alafoss Lopi in main shade A
1[1] ball of same in each of 3 contrast colours, B, C and D
One pair No 6/5mm needles
One pair No 3/6½mm needles
One No 6/5mm circular needle
One No 3/6½mm circular needle
The quantities of yarn given are based on average requirements and are approximate

Tension

13 sts and 16 rows to 4in/10cm over st st worked on No 3/6½mm needles

Back

With No 6/5mm needles and A, cast on 59[65] sts.
1st row (Rs) K1, *P1, K1, rep from * to end.
2nd row P1, *K1, P1, rep from * to end.
Rep these 2 rows for 3¼in/8cm, ending with a 1st row.
Next row (inc row) Rib 7[5], *M1 by picking up loop lying between needles and K tbl, rib 5[6], rep from * to last 2[0] sts, rib 2[0]. 69[75] sts.
Change to No 3/6½mm needles.

Beg with a K row, work 8 rows st st with A.
Cont working in st st from chart A for 9 rows.
Cont in st st with A only until back measures 16[17]in/41[43]cm from beg, ending with a Ws row.

Shape armholes

Cast off one st at beg of next 2 rows. 67[73] sts.
Leave rem sts on holder for yoke.

Front

Work as given for back until front measures 12 rows less than back to armhole shaping, ending with a Ws row.

Shape for yoke

1st row K across 26 sts, turn and P back, leaving rem sts on a spare needle for time being.
3rd row K across 20 sts, turn and P back, adding rem sts to spare needle.
5th row K across 14 sts, turn and P back adding rem sts to spare needle.
7th row K across 8 sts, turn and P back, adding rem sts to spare needle.
9th row K across 2 sts, turn and P back, adding rem sts to spare needle.
11th row K across all sts.
With Ws facing, shape other side of yoke by rep 1st to 11th rows,

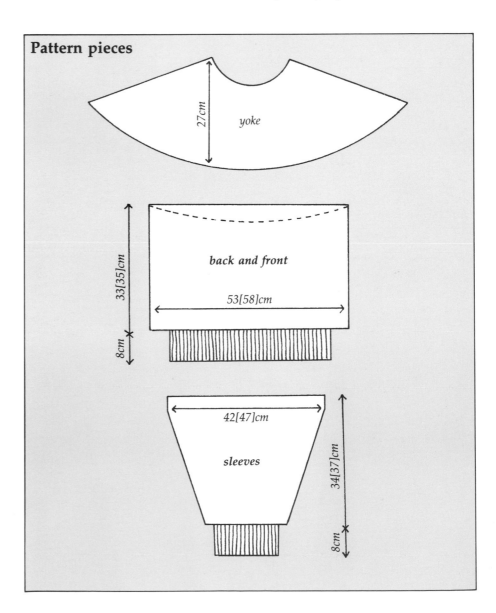

Pattern pieces

27cm

yoke

33[35]cm

8cm

back and front

53[58]cm

42[47]cm

sleeves

34[37]cm

8cm

112

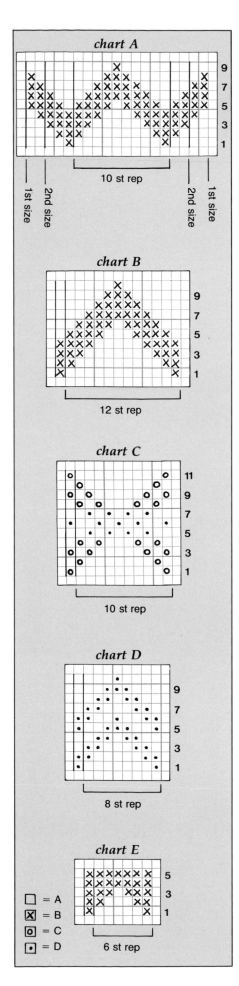

chart A

10 st rep

1st size | 2nd size | 2nd size | 1st size

chart B

12 st rep

chart C

10 st rep

chart D

8 st rep

chart E

6 st rep

□ = A
☒ = B
◉ = C
⊡ = D

reading P for K and K for P and ending with a Ws row. 69[75] sts.

Shape armholes
Cast off one st at beg of next 2 rows. 67[73] sts.

Sleeves
With No 6/5mm needles and A, cast on 25[31] sts.
Work in K1, P1 rib as given for back for 3¼in/8cm, ending with a 1st row.
Next row (inc row) Rib 3[1], *M1 as given for back, rib 2[3], rep from * to last 2[0] sts, rib 2[0]. 35[41] sts.
Change to No 3/6½mm needles. Beg with a K row work 8 rows st st with A, inc one st at each end of 3rd and foll 4th row. 39[45] sts.
Cont working in st st from chart A for 9 rows, still inc one st at each end of every 4th row, working extra sts into patt.
Cont in st st with A only, inc one st at each end of every 4th row until there are 55[61] sts.
Cont without shaping until sleeve measures 16½[17¾]in/42[45]cm from beg, ending with a Ws row.

Shape for underarm
Cast off one st at beg of next 2 rows. 53[59] sts.

Circular yoke
With Rs of work facing, sl first 33[36] sts from back on to holder. With Rs of work facing and No 3/6½mm circular needle, K across rem 34[37] sts of back, 53[59] sts of first sleeve, 67[73] sts from front, 53[59] sts of 2nd sleeve and 33[36] sts from back holder, inc one st in last st. 241[265] sts.
Mark last st with contrast coloured thread to denote end of round.
Cont in st st throughout, K each round, and work 10 rounds from chart B.
Next round (dec round) With A, *K2, (K2 tog, K4) 3 times, K2 tog, K2, rep from * to last st, K1. 201[221] sts.
Work 11 rounds from chart C.
Next round (dec round) With A, *K1, (K2 tog, K3) 3 times, K2 tog, K2, rep from * to last st, K1. 161[177] sts.
Work 10 rounds from chart D.
Next round (dec round) With A, *K1, (K2 tog, K2) 3 times, K2 tog,

K1, rep from * to last st, K1. 121[133] sts.
Work 5 rounds from chart E.
Next round (dec round) With B, *K2 tog, rep from * to last st, K1. 61[67] sts.
Work 4 more rounds with B.
Change to No 6/5mm circular needle and A. Work in rounds of K1, P1 rib for 2½in/6cm.
Cast off loosely in rib.

To make up
Press as directed on ball band, omitting ribbing.
Fold neckband in half to Ws and sl st down.
Join side and sleeve seams.

Icelandic jersey

This design features bands of coloured patterns which are reminiscent of Scandinavian motifs. It has been worked in an authentic Icelandic wool, in soft, muted colours.

The 'T' shape requires the minimum of increasing and decreasing, and the patterns are all worked over multiples of eight stitches.

Measurements

To fit 34–36[38–40]in/86–91[97–102]cm bust
Actual measurements, 41¾[45¾]in/106[116]cm
Length to shoulders, 26¾[27½]in/68[70] cm
Sleeve seam, 18[18½]in/46[47]cm
The figures in [] refer to the 38–40in/97–102cm size only

Materials

9[10] × 50g balls of Scotnord Alafoss Lyng in main shade A
2[3] balls of same in contrast colour B
3[4] balls of same in contrast colour C
One pair No 6/5mm needles
One pair No 3/6½mm needles
The quantities of yarn given are based on average requirements and are approximate

Tension

17 sts and 18 rows to 4in/10cm over patt worked on No 3/6½mm needles

Back

With No 6/5mm needles and A, cast on 77[85] sts.
1st row (Rs) K1, *P1, K1, rep from * to end.
2nd row P1, *K1, P1, rep from * to end.
Rep these 2 rows until back measures 3½in/9cm from beg, ending with a 1st row.
Next row (inc row) Rib 5[1] sts, *M1 by picking up loop lying between needles and K tbl, rib 6[7] sts, rep from * to end. 89[97] sts.

Change to No 3/6½mm needles.
Beg with a K row work in st st of 2 rows A, 2 rows B and 2 rows A.
Beg with a K row, cont working in patt from chart until back measures 25½[26¼]in/65[67]cm from beg, ending with a Ws row after working row 6, 14, 22 or 30 of chart.
Beg with a K row work in st st of 2 rows A, 2 rows B and 2 rows A.

Shape shoulders

With A, cast off 30[32] sts at beg of next 2 rows.
Leave rem 29[33] sts on holder for centre back neck.

Front

Work as given for back until front measures 23½[24¼]in/60[62]cm from beg, ending with a Ws row.

Shape neck

Next row Patt 37[39] sts, turn, leave rem sts on a spare needle.
Complete left shoulder first.
Dec one st at neck edge on next 3 rows, then on every alt row until 30[32] sts rem.
Cont without shaping until work measures same as back to shoulder, ending at armhole edge.
Cast off 30[32] sts.
With Rs of work facing, sl first 15[19] sts from spare needle on to holder and leave for centre front neck, rejoin yarn to rem sts and patt to end.
Complete right shoulder to match left, reversing shaping.

Sleeves

With No 6/5mm needles and A, cast on 35[43] sts. Work 2¾in/7cm rib as given for back welt, ending with a 1st row.
Next row (inc row) Rib 4[1] sts, *M1 as given for back, rib 2[3] sts, rep from * to last 3[0] sts, rib 3[0]. 49[57] sts.
Change to No 3/6½mm needles.
Beg with a K row work in st st of 2 rows A, 2 rows B and 2 rows A.
Beg with a K row, cont working in patt from chart, *at the same time* keep patt correct and inc one st at

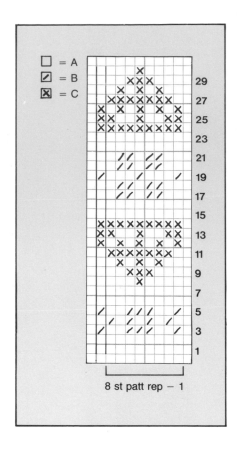

Pattern pieces

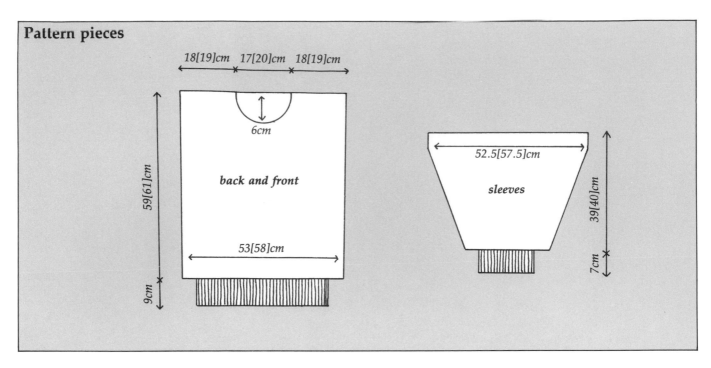

18[19]cm 17[20]cm 18[19]cm

6cm

back and front

59[61]cm

9cm

53[58]cm

52.5[57.5]cm

sleeves

39[40]cm

7cm

each end of next and every foll 3rd row until there are 89[97] sts, working extra sts into patt.
Cont without shaping until sleeve measures 17[17¼]in/43[44] cm from beg, ending with a Ws row after working row 6, 14, 22 or 30 of chart.
Beg with a K row work in st st of 2 rows A, 2 rows B and 2 rows A. With A, cast off loosely.

Neckband

Join right shoulder seam.
With Rs of work facing, No 6/5mm needles and A, pick up and K15 sts down left side of front neck, K across 15[19] front neck sts on holder, pick up and K15 sts up right front neck and K across 29[33] back neck sts on holder. 74[82] sts.
Work 2¼in/6cm in K1,P1 rib.
Cast off loosely in rib.

To make up

Press as directed on ball band, omitting ribbing.
Join left shoulder and neckband seam. Fold neckband in half to Ws and sl st down.
Fold sleeves in half lengthways, place fold to shoulder seam and sew in sleeves.
Join side and sleeve seams.

Helping hand

Whether you are using sets of needles or a circular needle, it is very easy to lose track of the beginning of each round particularly when working a coloured pattern.

To mark this point, use a slip loop of contrast coloured yarn and place it on the needle at the beginning of the first round. Each time you come to the end of a round, slip this loop from one needle point to the other without working into it.

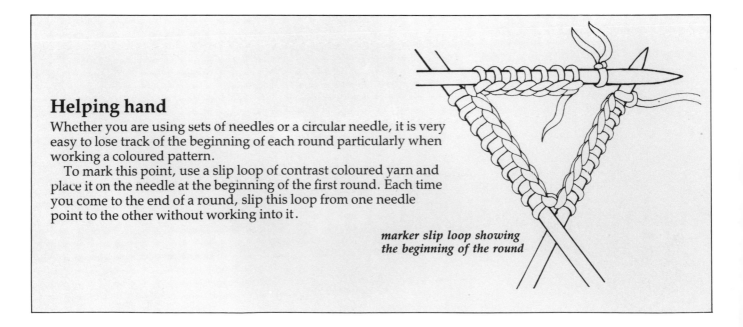

marker slip loop showing the beginning of the round

Falkland Islands knitting

The rugged terrain surrounding Port Stanley in this
nineteenth century engraving is typical of the Falkland Islands.
Since the days of the earliest settlers, the economy of the Islands
has been almost wholly based on sheep farming.
Although raw wool used to be exported the Islanders
are now spinning their own wool.

Falkland Islands knitting

The Falkland Islands lie about four hundred and eighty miles north-east of Cape Horn and four hundred miles off the coast of South America. The group consists of some two hundred islands, the largest being East Falkland and West Falkland, and their total land mass is some four thousand seven hundred square miles.

The Falkland Islands also have as their Dependencies, South Georgia, the South Sandwich Islands, the Shag Rocks and Clerke Rocks. South Georgia lies eight hundred miles east-south-east of the Falklands and the South Sandwich Islands about four hundred and seventy miles further south. These Dependencies are British territories but, for convenience, they are administered by the Falkland Islands government. A magistrate, who is also the Base Commander of the British Antarctic Survey Station, lives at King Edward Point in South Georgia, where there has been a government station since the beginning of the twentieth century, providing a base for Britain's long-standing interests in the Southern Hemisphere.

The uninhabited Falkland Islands were first discovered by a British sailor, Captain John Davis, in the 'Desire' in 1592. This event is commemorated in the motto of the Islands, 'Desire the Right'. The first known landing was in 1690 by Captain John Strong, who gave the Islands their name after Viscount Falkland, then Treasurer of the Navy. In 1764 a small colony was established by the French at Port Louis in East Falkland. Three years later the settlement was handed over to Spain for a modest sum of money. In the meantime, a British Captain, John Byron, made a comprehensive survey of West Falkland and in 1765 gave the name, Port Egmont, to an anchorage in Saunders Island. In the following year, a British settlement of about one hundred people was established at Port Egmont and the Islands were continuously inhabited by settlers from Britain until the formal colony was set up in 1833.

The terrain of the Islands is generally hilly, the highest points being Mount Usborne in East Falkland and Mount Adam in West Falkland, and the coastline is deeply indented, affording good anchorages. The uplands are almost bare of vegetation and consist of eroded peat, scree and ravines of quartize boulders, known as 'stone runs'. The climate is inhospitable and there are few trees, most of the vegetation consisting of grassland, heath and shrubs. Since the days of the earliest settlers, the economy of the Falkland Islands has been almost wholly based on sheep farming, producing wool, skins and hide

for export and meat as a local food supply. The grassland, which covers an extensive area, makes for excellent grazing and the hardy flocks of sheep were predominantly cross-bred from Corriedale, Romney and Polwarth strains.

In the past, the wool yield was exported as raw wool and it can only be assumed that any knitting on the Islands was intended for home use. Any knitting traditions would almost certainly be British, based on fishermens' garments and patterns, and coloured patterns similar to the examples obtained with natural colours in Iceland. Because the Islands were not on regular sailing routes, outside contact would have been very limited and there would have been no exchange of patterns or ideas. Knitting would have been considered as a local industry, providing warm and practical clothing for the population, but with no written or visual evidence of the type of knitting produced, it is impossible to lay any sort of claim to a history of knitting in the Islands.

Until quite recently the exports of raw wool were processed mainly in Britain, and then blended with other qualities to produce Aran and Shetland-type yarns. Much has been done in the past twenty years to increase wool production and present it as a speciality quality in its own right. The wool which is soft and resilient, free of vegetable contamination and very white, was originally sent to Britain to be spun and marketed. With the building of the first ever spinning mill on the Falklands at Fox Bay, West Falkland, the Islanders hope to take advantage of their reputation for producing exceptionally fine wool. Two years have been spent developing the wool and a new semi-worsted spinning process has given the product a unique softness and bulk.

The knitting patterns being used in the designs now produced in the Falklands cannot claim to be traditional in the region, but they are forming the foundation of a folk craft in a long-forgotten area. Only the meanings of the original British patterns are becoming representative of the way of life in the Islands. Cables are being used to represent the closeness of family life; moss stitch depicts the scree and peat of the uplands and coloured patterns are being introduced to reflect the natural colouring of the Islands.

This section continues with instructions for working some of these patterns and then goes on to feature two exclusive designs made in authentic Falkland Islands wool.

Falkland Islands patterns

Variations of moss stitch and cable patterns reflect the changes of terrain and the closeness of the community. Coloured patterns are simple in design and rely on the softness of natural colours for their effect.

Single moss stitch

This well-known seeded pattern can be worked over any number of stitches.

To work with an even number of stitches.

1st row *K1, P1, rep from * to the end of the row.
2nd row *P1, K1, rep from * to the end of the row.
These 2 rows form the pattern.

To work with an odd number of stitches, repeat the first row only.

Double moss stitch

This variation of moss stitch is also known as Aran moss stitch. This example requires multiples of 4 stitches, eg 20.

1st row (Rs) *K2, P2, rep from * to the end of the row.
2nd row As 1st row.
3rd row *P2, K2, rep from * to the end of the row.
4th row As 3rd row.
These 4 rows form the pattern.

Cable link pattern

The centre of each link of this cable pattern is worked in moss stitch. This example is worked as a panel of 16 stitches against a reversed stocking stitch background.

1st row (Rs) P4, sl next 3 sts on to a cable needle and hold at back of work, K1 from left hand needle then P1, K1, P1 from cable needle, sl next st on to cable needle and hold at front of work, K1, P1, K1 from left hand needle then K1 from cable needle, P4.
2nd row K4, (P1, K1) 3 times, P2, K4.
3rd row P4, (K1, P1) 3 times, K2, P4.
Rep 2nd and 3rd rows once more.
6th row As 2nd row.
7th row P4, K1, P1, K3, P1, K2, P4.
8th row K4, P1, K1, P3, K1, P2, K4.
These 8 rows form the pattern.

Double cable pattern

Only the edge stitches of this cable pattern are twisted in opposite directions to form a wide panel. This example requires multiples of 12 stitches, plus 2, eg 38, to form an all-over pattern.

1st row (Rs) P2, *K10, P2, rep from * to the end.
2nd row K2, *P10, K2, rep from * to the end.
3rd row P2, *sl next 2 sts on to cable needle and hold at back of work, K2 from left hand needle then K2 from cable needle, K2, sl next 2 sts on to cable needle and hold at front of work, K2 from left hand needle then K2 from cable needle, P2, rep from * to the end.
4th row As 2nd row.
5th row As 1st row.
6th row As 2nd row.
7th row As 1st row.
8th row As 2nd row.
These 8 rows form the pattern.

Zigzag coloured pattern

This simple two-colour pattern can be introduced into almost any fabric, or used to define a larger coloured pattern. This example requires multiples of 8 stitches, plus 1, eg 33, and 2 colours coded as A and B.

1st row (Rs) *K1 B, K3 A, rep from * to last st, K1 B.
2nd row *P2 B, P1 A, P3 B, P1 A, P1 B, rep from * to last st, P1 B.
3rd row *K1 A, K3 B, rep from * to last st, K1 A.
4th row *P2 A, P1 B, P3 A, P1 B, P1 A, rep from * to last st, P1 A.
These 4 rows form the pattern.

Coloured pebble pattern

Another simple two-colour pattern that forms a narrow band. This example requires multiples of 8 stitches, plus 1, eg 33, and 2 colours coded as A and B.

1st row (Rs) With A, K to end.
2nd row P1 B, *P3 A, P1 B, rep from * to end.
3rd row K1 B, *K2 A, K3 B, K2 A, K1 B, rep from * to end.
4th row P1 B, *(P1 A, P2 B), twice, P1 A, P1 B, rep from * to end.
5th row As 3rd row.
6th row As 2nd row.
7th row As 1st row.
8th row With A, P to end.
These 8 rows form the pattern.

Helping hand

A double crew neckband which is folded in half to the inside of the garment gives a very neat and snug effect and is particularly suitable for chunky garments. If the neckband is stitched in place too tightly, however, it is difficult to pull the garment over the head.

   To overcome this, once the required length of neckband has been completed, leave the stitches on a needle instead of casting them off. Thread a blunt-ended sewing needle with a length of matching yarn and secure this at the lower edge of the first picked-up stitch of the neckband. Fold the neckband in half, then insert the sewing needle into the loop at the top of the same stitch on the needle and pull the yarn through loosely.

   *Now insert the sewing needle under one strand at the lower edge of the next stitch and pull the yarn through. Insert the sewing needle into the loop at the top of the same stitch on the needle and pull the yarn through loosely, (see Fig 1).

   Continue in this way from the * until all the loops have been fastened off from the needle. Finish off with one or two small running stitches.

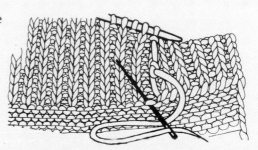

fig 1 completing a double crew neckband

Opposite: This striking jersey in an all-over coloured pattern is worked in pure Falkland wool , see pattern on page 124.
It was designed and made in the Falkland Islands by Jennifer Jones.

Jersey from the Falklands

This design is worked in bands of coloured patterns similar to Fair Isle designs. It was designed in the Falklands from wool spun locally. It has a dropped shoulder-line, so there is very little shaping, except for the round neck.

Measurements

To fit 34–36in/86–91cm bust/chest
Actual measurements, 42½in/108cm
Length to shoulder, 26¾in/68cm
Sleeve seam, 18½in/47cm

Materials

10 × 50g balls of Ponytown pure Falkland wool, Aran type, in main shade A
4 balls of same in contrast colour B
4 balls of same in contrast colour C
One pair No 8/4mm needles
One pair No 5/5½mm needles
The quantities of yarn given are based on average requirements and are approximate

Tension

19 sts and 20 rows to 4in/10cm over patt worked on No 5/5½mm needles

Back

With No 8/4mm needles and A, cast on 99 sts.

1st row (Rs) P1, *K1, P1, rep from * to end.
2nd row K1, *P1, K1, rep from * to end.
Cont in rib as given until work measures 4¾in/12cm from beg, ending with a Rs row.
Next row (inc row) Rib 9, *pick up loop lying between needles and K tbl — called M1 —, rib 16, rep from * to last 10 sts, M1, rib 10. 105 sts.
Change to No 5/5½mm needles.
Cont working patt from chart, beg with 1st row and when 86th row has been completed, rep patt from the 3rd row until the back measures 26¾in/68cm from beg, ending with a Ws row.

Shape shoulders

Keeping patt correct, cast off 18 sts at beg of next 4 rows. Leave rem 33 sts on holder for centre back neck.

Front

Work as given for back until front measures 22¾in/58cm from beg, ending with a Ws row.

Shape neck

Next row Patt 43 sts, turn and complete left shoulder first. Keeping patt correct throughout dec one st at neck edge on next and every foll alt row until 36 sts rem. Cont without shaping until work measures same as back to shoulder, ending with same patt row.

Shape shoulder

Cast off 18 sts at beg of next and foll alt row.
With Rs of work facing, sl next 19 sts on to holder and leave for centre front neck, rejoin yarn to rem sts and patt to end.
Complete right shoulder to match left, reversing shaping and noting that one extra row must be worked before beg shoulder shaping.

Sleeves

With No 8/4mm needles and A, cast on 43 sts. Work in rib as given for back until sleeve measures 3½in/9cm from beg, ending with a Rs row.
Next row (inc row) Rib 3, *M1, rib 4, rep from * to end. 53 sts.
Change to No 5/5½mm needles.
Cont working in patt from chart at the st indicated, *at the same time* inc one st at each end of 1st and every foll 3rd row until there are 105 sts. Cont without shaping until work measures 18½in/47cm from beg, (81st patt row), then P 1 row. Cast off.

Neckband

Join right shoulder seam. With Rs of work facing, No 8/4mm needles and A, pick up and K26 sts down left front neck, K across 19 sts on front neck holder, K up 26 sts up right front neck and K across 33 sts on back neck holder dec one st in centre. 103 sts.
Beg with a 2nd row, work in rib as given for back for 3½in/8cm. Cast off loosely in rib, using No 5/5½mm needle.

To make up

Press as directed on ball band, omitting ribbing.
Join left shoulder and neckband seam. Fold neckband in half to Ws and sl st down.
Place centre of cast off edge of sleeves to shoulder seams and sew in place. Join side and sleeve seams. Press seams.

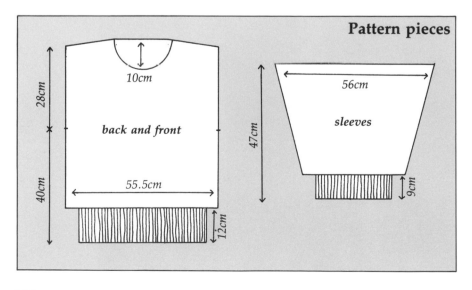

Pattern pieces

back and front — 10cm, 28cm, 40cm, 55.5cm, 12cm

sleeves — 56cm, 47cm, 9cm

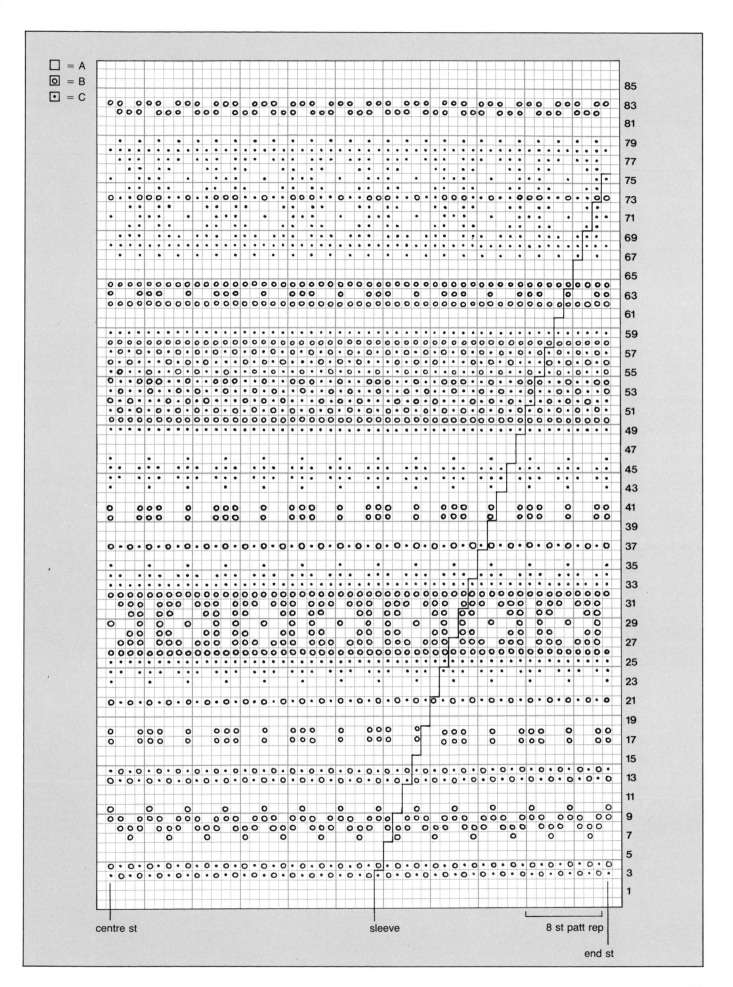

□ = A
◉ = B
⊡ = C

centre st   sleeve   8 st patt rep

end st

Jersey for the family

This jersey, knitted in authentic pure new wool, processed by the mill at Fox Bay in West Falkland, is reminiscent of fishermens' designs and incorporates cables and travelling stitches in the stitch patterns.
The sizes given cover a wide range, suitable for children, women and men. The garment features raglan sleeves for ease of movement and a neat, round neckline.

Measurements

To fit 24[26:28:30:32 – 34:36 – 38:40:42 – 44]in/60[65:70:75:80 – 86:91 – 97:101:107 – 112]cm bust/chest
Actual measurements, 25[29:32:35:38:42:45:48]in/64[72:81:88:96:105:113:121]cm
Length to back neck, excluding neckband, 16[18½:21:23:25:27:29:30]in/41[47:53:58:64:69:74:76]cm
Sleeve seam, 11½[13:13¾:15½:17:17¾:18½:18½]in/29[33:35:39:43:45:47:47]cm
The figures in [] refer to the 26/65, 28/70, 30/75, 32 – 34/80 – 86, 36 – 38/91 – 97, 40/101 and 42 – 44in/107 – 112cm sizes respectively

Materials

8[10:12:15:17:19:22:24] × 50g balls of The Falkland Mill Aran Type 100% Falkland wool, distributed by Ponytown Ltd
One pair No 9/3¾mm needles
One pair No 6/5mm needles
Cable needle
The quantities of yarn given are based on average requirements and are approximate

Tension

18 sts and 24 rows to 4in/10cm over st st worked on No 6/5mm needles

Note

To mark with a slip marker, make a slip knot in a short length of contrasting yarn and place on needle where indicated. On the following rows slip the marker from one needle to the other until the pattern is established and the marker is no longer required

Pattern panel

Worked over 50[50:50:50:82:82:82:82] sts between markers on back and front and 34 sts between markers on sleeves.
On the back and front, work the instructions given in round brackets 2[2:2:2:4:4:4:4] times, in addition to the sts on either side.
1st row (Rs) P7, sl next 2 sts on to cable needle and hold at back of work, K2 from left hand needle then K2 from cable needle — abbreviated as C4B —, (P5, sl next st on to cable needle and hold at front of work, K into back of next st on left hand needle then K into back of st on cable needle — abbreviated as C2F —, P5, C4B), P7.
2nd row K7, P4, (K5, P into back of next 2 sts — abbreviated as P2B —, K5, P4), K7.
3rd row P6, sl next st on to cable needle and hold at back of work, K2 from left hand needle then P1 from cable needle — abbreviated as T3B —, sl next 2 sts on to cable needle and hold at front of work, P1 from left hand needle then K2 from cable needle — abbreviated as T3F —, (P3, sl next st on to cable needle and hold at back of work, K1 tbl from left hand needle then P1 from cable needle — abbreviated as T2B —, sl next st on to cable needle and hold at front of work, P1 from left hand needle then K1 tbl from cable needle — abbreviated as T2F —, P3, T3B, T3F), P6.
4th row K6, P2, K2, P2, (K3, P into back of next st — abbreviated as P1B —, K2, P1B, K3, P2, K2, P2), K6.
5th row P5, T3B, P2, T3F, (P2, K into back of next st — abbreviated as K1B —, P2, K1B, P2, T3B, P2, T3F), P5.
6th row K5, P2, K4, P2, (K2, P1B, K2, P1B, K2, P2, K4, P2), K5.

7th row P4, T3B, P1, K into back of next 2 sts — abbreviated as K2B —, P1, (T3F, P1, T2F, T2B, P1, T3B, P1, K2B, P1), T3F, P4.
8th row K4, P2, K2, P2B, (K2, P2, K2, P2B, K2, P2, K2, P2B), K2, P2, K4.
9th row P3, T3B, P1, T2B, T2F, (P1, T3F, P4, T3B, P1, T2B, T2F), P1, T3F, P3.
10th row K3, P2, K2, P1B, K2, P1B, (K2, P2, K4, P2, K2, P1B, K2, P1B), K2, P2, K3.
11th row P2, T3B, P2, K1B, P2, K1B, (P2, T3F, P2, T3B, P2, K1B, P2, K1B), P2, T3F, P2.
12th row K2, P2, K3, P1B, K2, P1B, (K3, P2, K2, P2, K3, P1B, K2, P1B), K3, P2, K2.
13th row P1, T3B, P3, T2F, T2B, (P3, T3F, T3B, P3, T2F, T2B), P3, T3F, P1.
14th row K1, P2, K5, P2B, (K5, P4, K5, P2B), K5, P2, K1.
15th row P1, K2, P5, C2F, (P5, C4B, P5, C2F), P5, K2, P1.
16th row As 14th row.
17th row P1, T3F, P3, T2B, T2F, (P3, T3B, T3F, P3, T2B, T2F), P3, T3B, P1.
18th row As 12th row.
19th row P2, T3F, P2, K1B, P2, K1B, (P2, T3B, P2, T3F, P2, K1B, P2, K1B), P2, T3B, P2.
20th row As 10th row.
21st row P3, T3F, P1, T2F, T2B, (P1, T3B, P1, K2B, P1, T3F, P1, T2F, T2B), P1, T3B, P3.
22nd row As 8th row.
23rd row P4, T3F, P4, (T3B, P1, T2B, T2F, P1, T3F, P4), T3B, P4.
24th row As 6th row.
25th row P5, T3F, P2, (T3B, P2, K1B, P2, K1B, P2, T3F, P2), T3B, P5.
26th row As 4th row.
27th row P6, T3F, T3B, (P3, T2F, T2B, P3, T3F, T3B), P6.
28th row As 2nd row.
These 28 rows form pattern panel.

*Opposite: Cables and travelling patterns have been used on this raglan-sleeved jersey, which is in a wide size range suitable for all the family.
Worked in authentic Falkland wool and designed by Lyric Patterns.*

Pattern pieces

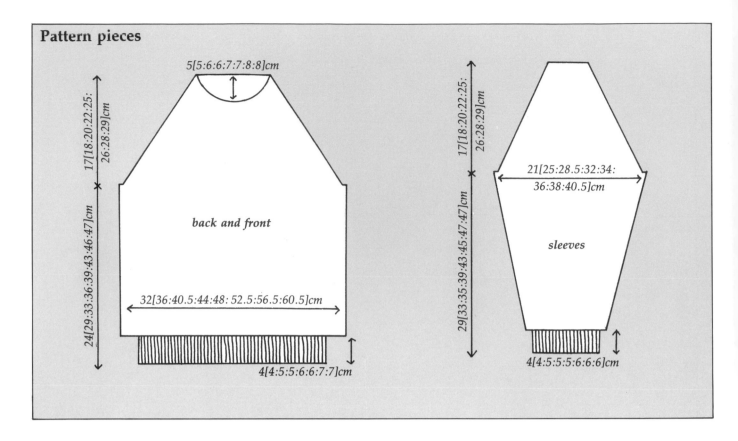

back and front

5[5:6:6:7:7:8:8]cm

17[18:20:22:25: 26:28:29]cm

24[29:33:36:39:43:46:47]cm

32[36:40.5:44:48: 52.5:56.5:60.5]cm

4[4:5:5:6:6:7:7]cm

sleeves

21[25:28.5:32:34: 36:38:40.5]cm

17[18:20:22:25: 26:28:29]cm

29[33:35:39:43:45:47:47]cm

4[4:5:5:5:6:6:6]cm

Back

With No 9/3¾mm needles cast on 58[66:74:82:88:96:104:112] sts. Work 9[9:11:11:13:13:15:15] rows K1, P1 rib.
Next row (inc row) Rib 3[7:11:15:6:10:14:18] sts, *inc in next st, rib 2[2:2:2:3:3:3:3] sts, rep from * to last 4[8:12:16:6:10:14:18] sts, inc in next st, rib to end. 76[84:92:100:108:116:124:132] sts. Change to No 6/5mm needles. Commence patt as foll:
1st row (Rs) (K1B, P1) 4[6:8:10:4:6:8:10] times, P1, K into front of 2nd st on left hand needle then K into front of first st, slipping both sts off needle tog — abbreviated as C2R —, K into back of 2nd st on left hand needle then K into front of first st, slipping both sts off needle tog — abbreviated as C2L —, place slip marker, work 1st row of patt panel across next 50[50:50:50:82:82:82:82] sts, place slip marker, C2R, C2L, P2, K1B, (P1, K1B) 3[5:7:9:3:5:7:9] times.
2nd row K9[13:17:21:9:13:17:21], P4, work 2nd row of patt panel over sts as set, P4, K9[13:17:21:9:13:17:21].
3rd row (K1B, P1) 4[6:8:10:4:6:8:10] times, P1, C2L, C2R, work 3rd row of patt panel over sts as set, C2L,

C2R, P2, K1B, (P1, K1B) 3[5:7:9:3:5:7:9] times.
4th row K9[13:17:21:9:13:17:21], P4, work 4th row of patt panel over sts as set, P4, K9[13:17:21:9:13:17:21].
These 4 rows form the patt for the sts at each end of rows.
Keeping the 28 rows of central patt panel correct on sts between markers, rep last 4 rows until back measures 9½[11½:13:14:15¼: 16¾:18¼:18½]in/ 24[29:33:36:39:43:46:47]cm from beg, ending with a Ws row.

Shape raglans
**Keeping patt correct throughout cast off one st at beg of next 2 rows.
3rd row K2, P2 tog, patt to last 4 sts, P2 tog, K2.
4th row P3, patt to last 3 sts, P3.**
Rep last 2 rows until 36[38:40:42:48:54:60:66] sts rem, ending with a Ws row.
Next row K2, P3 tog, patt to last 5 sts, P3 tog, K2. 2 sts dec each end of row.
Next row P3, patt to last 3 sts, P3.
Rep last 2 rows until 24[26:28:30:32:34:36:38] sts rem, ending with a dec row.
Next row P1[2:3:4:5:1:2:3], *P2 tog, P3, rep from * to last

3[4:5:6:7:3:4:5] sts, P2 tog, P to end.
Sl rem 19[21:23:25:27:27:29:31] sts on to holder and leave for centre back neck.

Front

Work as given for back to second **.
Rep last 2 rows until 42[44:46:48:54:60:66:72] sts rem, ending with a dec row.

Shape neck
Next row Keeping patt correct throughout, work 17[17:18:19:22:25:28:31] sts, (P2 tog, P1[2:2:2:2:2:2:2] sts) twice, P2 tog, work 1[1:2:3:3:3:3:3] sts, slip the last 7[9:11:13:13:13:13:13] just worked on to holder and work to end on rem 16[16:16:16:19:22:25:28] sts.
Complete this side first.
Cont to dec at raglan edge on next and every foll alt row as before, *at the same time* dec one st at neck edge on next 5 rows.
8[8:8:8:11:14:17:20] sts.
Work one row without shaping.
Next row K2, P3 tog, patt to last 2 sts, P2 tog.
Work one row without shaping.

128

5th, 6th, 7th and 8th sizes only
Rep last 2 rows 1[2:3:4] times
more.

All sizes
Work as foll on rem 5 sts.
Next row K2, P3 tog.
Dec one st at neck edge only on
foll alt row. Cast off.
With Rs of work facing, rejoin
yarn to neck edge of rem
16[16:16:16:19:22:25:28] sts and
complete to match first side,
reversing shapings.

Sleeves

With No 9/3¾mm needles cast on
32[34:36:38:42:44:46:48] sts. Work
9[9:11:11:11:13:13:13] rows K1, P1
rib.
Next row (inc row) Rib
3[2:5:4:4:2:6:4], *inc in next st, rib
1[1:1:1:2:2:2:2] sts, rep from * to
last 3[2:5:4:5:3:7:5] sts, inc in next
st, rib to end.
46[50:50:54:54:58:58:62] sts.
Change to No 6/5mm needles.
Commence patt.
1st row (Rs) (K1B, P1)
1[2:2:3:3:4:4:5] times, C2R, C2L,
place slip marker, work 1st row of
pattern panel across next 34 sts,
place slip marker, C2R, C2L, (P1,
K1B) 1[2:2:3:3:4:4:5] times.

2nd row K2[4:4:6:6:8:8:10], P4,
work 2nd row of pattern panel as
now set, P4, K to end.
3rd row (K1B, P1) 1[2:2:3:3:4:4:5]
times, C2L, C2R, work 3rd row of
pattern panel as now set, C2L,
C2R, (P1, K1B) 1[2:2:3:3:4:4:5]
times.
4th row K2[4:4:6:6:8:8:10], P4,
work 4th row of pattern panel as
now set, P4, K to end.
These 4 rows form the patt for the
sts at each end of rows.
Keeping the 28 rows of central patt
panel correct on sts between
markers, rep the last 4 rows, *at the
same time* inc one st at each end of
foll 8th [8th:8th:4th:4th:4th:4th:
4th] row and every foll
13th[13th:7th:7th:6th:6th:5th:5th]
row until there are
54[60:68:76:80:84:88:92] sts,
working extra sts into K1B, P1 patt
at each end.
Cont without shaping until sleeve
measures 11½[13:13¾:15¼:17:
17¾:18½:18½]in/
29[33:35:39:43:45:47:47]cm from
beg, ending with a Ws row.

Shape raglan
Work as given for back from ** to
**.
Rep last 2 rows until

8[8:10:12:12:12:12:12] sts rem,
ending with dec row.
Next row P2[2:3:4:4:4:4:4], (P2 tog)
twice, P2[2:3:4:4:4:4:4].
Sl rem 6[6:8:10:10:10:10:10] sts on
to holder.

Neckband
Join raglan seams, leaving right
back raglan open.
With Rs of work facing and No
9/3¾mm needles, K across sts on
back neck holder and left sleeve
top holder, pick up and
K9[11:11:11:13:15:17:19] sts down
left side of front neck, K across
front neck sts on holder, pick up
and K9[11:11:11:13:15:17:19] sts up
right side of front neck and K
across sts on right sleeve top
holder. 56[64:72:80:86:90:96:102]
sts.
Work 2½[2½:3:3:3:3:3:3]in/
6[6:8:8:8:8:8:8]cm in K1, P1 rib.
Cast off very loosely in rib.

To make up
Press as directed on ball band,
omitting ribbing.
Join rem raglan seam and ends of
neckband. Fold neckband in half
to Ws and sl st down.
Join side and sleeve seams.

Abbreviations, conversions and needle sizes

Knitting abbreviations

alt	alternate(ly)
approx	approximate(ly)
beg	begin(ning)
cont	continu(e)(ing)
cm	centimetre(s)
dec	decrease
foll	follow(ing)
g st	garter stitch, every row knit
g	gramme(s)
in	inch(es)
inc	increase
K	knit
K up	pick up and knit
K-wise	in a knitwise direction
mm	millimetre(s)
No	number
patt	pattern
psso	pass slipped stitch over
P	purl
P up	pick up and purl
P-wise	in a purlwise direction
rem	remain(ing)
rep	repeat
Rs	right side of work
sl	slip
sl st	slip stitch
st(s)	stitch(es)
st st	stocking stitch, 1 row knit, 1 row purl
tbl	through back of loop
tog	together
Ws	wrong side of work
ybk	yarn back between needles
yfwd	yarn forward between needles
yon	yarn over needle
yrn	yarn round needle

Knitting symbols

Where an asterisk, *, is shown in a row, it means that the stitches given after this sign must be repeated from that point to the end of the row, or to the last number of stitches given. Where a double asterisk is shown, **, it means that this part of the pattern will be used at a later stage on another section of the garment.

Instructions shown in square brackets, [], denote larger sizes respectively.

Instructions shown in round brackets, ( ), mean that this section of the pattern is worked on all sizes.

Knitting yarn weight conversions

25g balls	oz balls	25g balls	oz balls
1	1	13	11
3	2	14	12
4	3	15	13
5	4	16	14
6	5	17	15
7	6	18	16
8	7	19	17
9	8	21	18
10	9	22	19
12	10	23	20

Knitting needle sizes

Old British	Metric	UK Metric	American
000	10mm		15
00	9mm		13
0	8mm		12
1	7.5mm	7½mm	11
2	7mm		10½
3	6.5mm	6½mm	10
4	6mm		9
5	5.5mm	5½mm	8
6	5mm		7
7	4.5mm	4½mm	6
8	4mm		5
9	3.75mm	3¾mm	4
10	3.25mm	3¼mm	3
11	3mm		2
12	2.75mm	2¾mm	1
13	2.25mm	2¼mm	0
14	2mm		00

Circular needle chart

The following information shows the minimum number of stitches required to reach from one needle point to the other.

Tension	Needle length			
	16in/ 40cm	24in/ 60cm	32in/ 80cm	40in/ 100cm
5 sts to 1 in/2.5cm	80	116	156	196
5½ sts to 1 in/2.5cm	88	128	172	216
6 sts to 1 in/2.5cm	96	140	188	236
6½ sts to 1 in/2.5cm	104	152	204	254
7 sts to 1 in/2.5cm	112	164	220	274
7½ sts to 1 in/2.5cm	120	176	236	294
8 sts to 1 in/2.5cm	128	188	252	314

Helping
hand

Helping hand

If you have never knitted before or have let your skills become rusty, the following step-by-step instructions and explanatory diagrams will help you discover this craft for the first time, or will rekindle your enthusiasm.

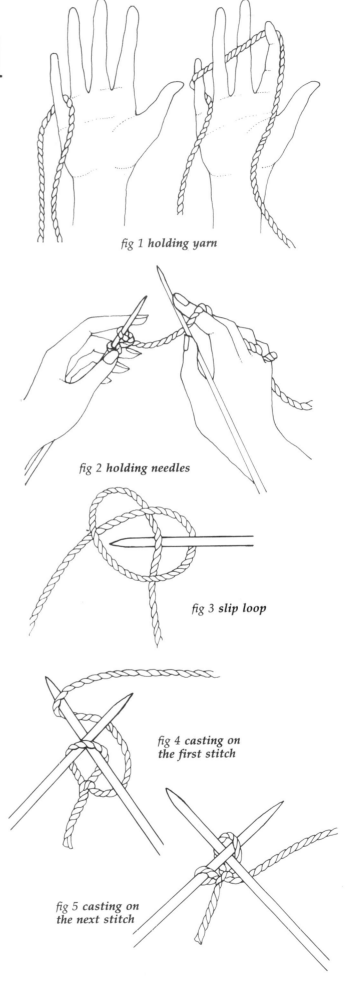

fig 1 *holding yarn*

Holding yarn and needles

Use these methods as a guide until you find a way of holding the yarn and needles which suits you. It is essential to be comfortable and relaxed or you will not produce an even fabric.

Right handed knitters should hold the yarn wound round the fingers of the right hand, in such a way as to achieve a firm fabric, (see Fig 1). The needle making the stitches is held in the right hand and the left hand needle holds the made stitches, (see Fig 2).

These illustrations are for right handed knitters. If you are left handed, prop the book up in front of you so that it is facing a mirror and work from the reflection.

fig 2 *holding needles*

Making a slip loop

All knitting begins with a slip loop, which counts as the first cast on stitch.

To make a slip loop, take the main end from the ball of yarn across in front of the short end and use the point of the needle to pull the main length through from the back to the front and leave this loop on the needle, (see Fig 3). Draw up the main length to tighten the knot.

fig 3 *slip loop*

Casting on

The simplest method of casting on uses two needles. Hold the needle with the slip loop on it in your left hand and the other needle in your right hand, with the yarn wound round your fingers.

Insert the point of the right hand needle into the slip loop from the front to the back and take the yarn under and round the point, (see Fig 4). Draw the yarn through the slip loop to make a new stitch and place this stitch on the left hand needle.

*Make the next stitch by inserting the point of the right hand needle from the front to the back between the last two stitches on the left hand needle, (see Fig 5). Take the yarn under and round the point of the right hand needle and draw the yarn through to make another stitch. Place this stitch on the left hand needle.

Continue repeating from the * until you have cast on the required number of stitches.

fig 4 *casting on the first stitch*

fig 5 *casting on the next stitch*

To knit stitches

To knit the first row after casting on, hold the needle containing the cast on stitches in your left hand and the yarn and spare needle in your right hand.

*Insert the point of the right hand needle through the first stitch on the left hand needle from the front to the back. Holding the yarn at the back of the work, take it under and over the point of the right hand needle and draw a loop through the stitch on the left hand needle, (see Fig 6). Keep this newly made stitch on the right hand needle and allow the stitch knitted into to drop off the left hand needle. One stitch has been knitted.

Repeat this action from the * into each stitch until all the stitches have been worked on to the right hand needle. One row has been knitted. To work the next row, transfer the needle holding the stitches to your left hand, so that the yarn is again in the correct position at the beginning of the row.

Working consecutive knitted rows in this way produces the fabric called 'garter stitch', which is closely-textured and ridged.

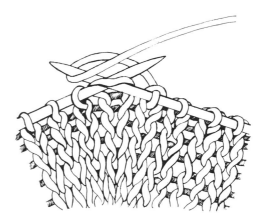

fig 6 *to knit stitches*

To purl stitches

Hold the needle containing the cast on, or knitted stitches in your left hand and the yarn and spare needle in your right hand.

*Insert the point of the right hand needle through the first stitch on the left hand needle from the right to the left. Holding the yarn at the front of the work, take it over and round the point of the right hand needle and draw a loop through the stitch on the left hand needle, (see Fig 7). Keep this newly made stitch on the right hand needle and allow the stitch purled into to drop off the left hand needle. One stitch has been purled.

Repeat this action from the * into each stitch until all the stitches have been worked on to the right hand needle. One row has been purled. To work the next row, transfer the needle holding the stitches to your left hand, so that the yarn is again in the correct position at the beginning of the row.

Knitting the first (right side) row and purling the second (wrong side) row, and continuing to alternate the rows in this way produces stocking stitch, the smoothest of all knitted fabrics. The purl side of this fabric is referred to as 'reversed stocking stitch'.

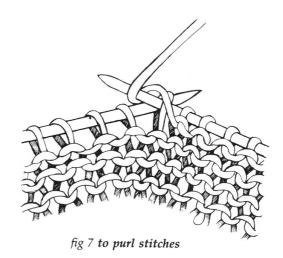

fig 7 *to purl stitches*

To shape by increasing

Where instructions state that one stitch is to be increased at the beginning, end, or at each end of a particular row as a means of shaping, the easiest method is to work twice into a stitch, thus making two out of one.

To make a stitch at the beginning of a knit row, work the first stitch in the usual way but do not allow the stitch to drop off the left hand needle. Instead, insert the right hand needle into the back loop of the same stitch and knit into it again, (see Fig. 8).

fig 8 *increasing a knit stitch*

To make a stitch at the end of a knit row, work until two stitches remain on the left hand needle. Increase in the next stitch as given for the beginning of the row, then work the last stitch in the usual way to keep the edge straight.

To make a stitch at the beginning of a purl row, work the first stitch in the usual way but do not allow the stitch to drop off the left hand needle. Instead, insert the right hand needle into the back loop of the same stitch but from the left to the right, and purl into it again, (see Fig 9).

To make a stitch at the end of a purl row, work until two stitches remain on the left hand needle. Increase in the next stitch as given for the beginning of the row, then work the last stitch in the usual way to keep the edge straight.

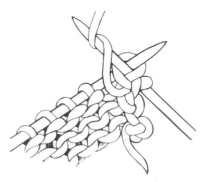

fig 9 increasing a purl stitch

Decorative eyelet increasing

This method forms an eyelet hole in the fabric and is the basis of all lace knitting. Instead of knitting into a stitch to make an extra one, the yarn is taken over or round the needle to increase a stitch and this stitch is compensated for by decreasing a stitch later on in the pattern sequence.

To make a stitch between two knitted stitches, bring the yarn forward between the needles, then take it back over the top of the right hand needle ready to knit the next stitch, (see Fig. 10). This is called 'yarn forward'.

To make a stitch between a purled and knitted stitch, the yarn is already at the front of the work and should be carried over the top of the right hand needle ready to knit the next stitch, (see Fig 11). This is called 'yarn over (or on) needle'.

To make a stitch between a knitted and a purled stitch, bring the yarn forward between the needles to the front of the work, take it over the top of the right hand needle and round between the needles again ready to purl the next stitch, (see Fig 12). This is called 'yarn round needle'.

This method is also used to make a stitch between two purled stitches, noting that the yarn is already at the front of the work to begin, and should be taken over the top of the right hand needle and round between the needles ready to purl the next stitch.

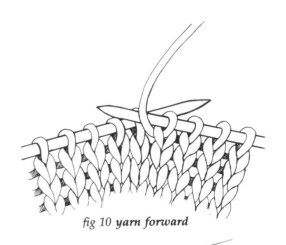

*fig 10 **yarn forward***

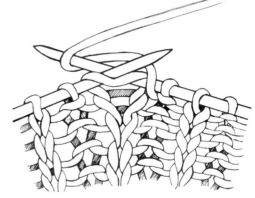

*fig 11 **yarn over needle***

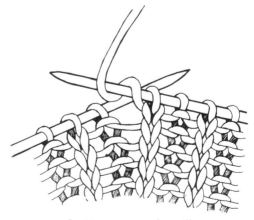

*fig 12 **yarn round needle***

To shape by decreasing

Where instructions state that one stitch is to be decreased at the beginning, end, or at each end of a particular row as a means of shaping, the easiest method is to work two stitches together, thus making one out of two.

To decrease a stitch at the beginning of a knit row, insert the point of the right hand needle from the front to the back through the first two stitches on the left hand needle, instead of through one stitch, and knit them together in the usual way, allowing both stitches to drop off the left hand needle, (see Fig 13).

To decrease a stitch at the end of a knit row, work until three stitches remain on the left hand needle. Decrease in the next two stitches as given for the beginning of the row, then work the last stitch in the usual way to keep the edge straight.

The methods for decreasing a stitch at the beginning or end of a purl row are the same as for a knit row, but the decreased stitches are purled together, inserting the right hand needle from right to left through two stitches.

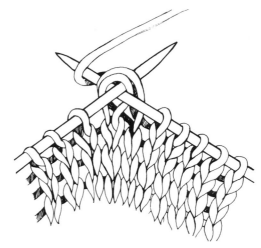

fig 13 *decreasing one stitch*

Casting off

This method is used to stop the stitches unravelling at the end of a completed section of knitting, or for certain areas of shaping in a section, such as necklines and shoulders. When casting off, make sure that the stitches are worked in the correct pattern sequence before they are cast off, or you will spoil the appearance of the fabric and make seaming more difficult.

To cast off stitches at the beginning of a row, work the first two stitches in pattern and leave them on the right hand needle. *Insert the point of the left hand needle into the first of the stitches worked on to the right hand needle and lift it over the top of the second stitch and off the needle, leaving one stitch on the right hand needle, (see Fig 14). Work the next stitch in pattern and leave it on the right hand needle and continue from the * until the correct number of stitches have been cast off.

If casting off is at the end of a piece of knitting, break off the yarn, draw it through the remaining stitch on the right hand needle and pull it up securely. If stitches have been cast off as a means of shaping, continue in pattern to the end of the row, noting that the stitch on the right hand needle now counts as one of the remaining stitches.

To cast off stitches in the middle of a row, work in pattern until the position for the shaping is reached, continue as given for the beginning of the row until the required number of stitches have been cast off. Pattern to the end of the row, noting that the stitch on the right hand needle now counts as one of the remaining stitches.

To cast off stitches at the end of a row, work in pattern until the number of stitches to be cast off remain on the left hand needle. Cast off these stitches and fasten off as given for the beginning of the row. To continue working on the remaining stitches, rejoin the yarn again to the beginning of the next row.

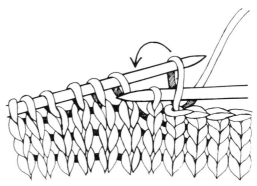

fig 14 *casting off*

Knitting tension

Knitting is an easy craft to master but you will not become a proficient exponent until you understand the importance of obtaining the correct tension given for a design. Many knitters believe this term means achieving an even fabric, but this is not so, although it certainly contributes to the appearance of your knitting.

The word 'tension' refers to the number of stitches and rows to a given measurement, usually 4in (10cm), which have been achieved by the *designer* of the garment, using the yarn and needle size quoted in the instructions. Without doubt, correct tension is the factor which makes the difference between successful and calamitous results, as it controls the size and shape of the design.

Each yarn manufacturer gives a recommended tension and needle size on the ball band of the qualities they produce, but this is only a guide to obtaining a *stocking stitch* fabric which is neither too tight nor too loose. As soon as you begin to work in a stitch pattern, however, this basic tension will no longer apply and the tension given in the designer's instructions will differ from those given on the ball band.

Whether you are a novice or an experienced knitter, each time you begin to knit a garment it is vital to first work a tension sample, using the correct yarn and needle size given in the instructions, to ensure that you obtainthe same number of stitches and rows quoted under the 'Tension' heading. Some people naturally knit more tightly, or loosely than others and everyone differs in the way they control the yarn and needles. To begin with, there is no such thing as an 'average' tension and as you gain experience, your tension may alter with your progress.

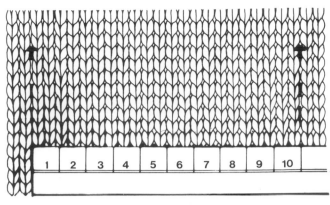

fig 15 checking tension sample

To adjust knitting tension

To adjust your tension, simply change needle sizes and work another sample. If your original sample measures *more* than the size given you are working too *loosely* and you must change to a size smaller needles. If your original sample measures *less* than the size given you are working too *tightly* and must change to a size larger needles. Experiment with different sizes until you can obtain the correct tension—it doesn't matter how many times you have to change needles. Most garments are knitted so that the stitches form the width tension and the rows the length. If you have to choose between obtaining one or the other, the width tension is the most vital and length can be adjusted by working more or less rows to achieve the given measurement.

Always use new yarn to work each tension sample. If you keep unravelling the same yarn it will become stretched and will not give an accurate tension. If you are substituting another yarn for the one given in the instructions, it is even more essential to check your tension. In using a different yarn from the original quoted, you may also find that the amount required will vary and you may not be able to produce the texture of the original fabric.

To check knitting tension

Always work a sample of at least 4in (10cm) using the yarn, needle size and stitch pattern given in the instructions. If the tension is given as 22 stitches and 30 rows to 4in (10cm) worked in stocking stitch on No 8 (4mm) needles, cast on at least 26 stitches and work 34 rows, to enable you to measure the sample accurately.

Lay the completed sample on a flat surface and pin it down at the corners, without stretching it. Place a firm ruler across the knitting and mark out the number of stitches and rows you have obtained to 4in (10cm) with pins, (see Fig 15). Count the stitches and rows very carefully, as even half a stitch makes a great deal of difference to the finished size of the garment.

Blocking and pressing

Many of the yarns available today are completely ruined if they are pressed, so do check the spinner's recommendation on the ball band.

Where pressing is advised, it is easier if each section is first pinned out to the correct measurements and shape — this is particularly important in lace knitting. This is referred to as 'blocking', (see Fig 16). Use a firm, well-padded surface and place each section right side down on to this, securing each corner with rustless pins. Gently pat the section into size and shape, making sure that the side edges are

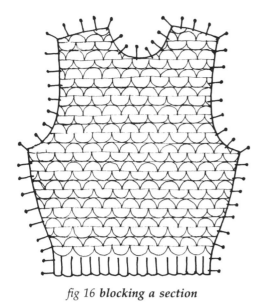

fig 16 blocking a section

straight and that the stitches and rows run in straight lines. Check that the measurements are the same as those given in the instructions, or as shown in the pattern pieces diagram. Now pin the section evenly to the padded surface round all the edges.

To press each section, have the iron at the correct temperature and a clean dry, or damp, cloth as directed in the instructions or on the ball band. Place the cloth over the section and gently press the whole area of the iron down on top of the cloth, then lift it up again. Do not run the iron over the surface of the cloth as you would if you were ironing, as this will stretch the knitting. Press each area in this way and when the section is completed, remove the pins and lay it aside ready for seaming.

Making up garments

When the various sections have been completed and pressed, it is the final seaming and finishing touches which will give your garments a professional look.

Seaming

To join the sections together, the best method to use is a back stitch seam. Unless it is very thick, or highly-textured, the yarn used to knit the garment should be used for seaming.

Place the right sides of each piece together and sew along the wrong side of the fabric, about ¼in (0.5cm) in from the edge. Thread a length of yarn into a blunt-ended sewing needle. Working from right to left along the seam, secure the yarn at the end with a few small running stitches.

*With the sewing needle at the back of the work, move it to the left about the width of one knitted

stitch, push it through to the front of the work and pull the yarn through. Take the needle across the front of the work from left to right and insert it through the fabric at the end of the last stitch, then pull the yarn through, (see Fig 17).

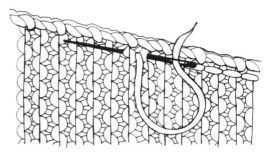

fig 17 back stitch seam

Continue working from the * in this way until the seam is completed, then fasten off at the end with a few small running stitches.

Picking up stitches

Necklines and borders need to be neatened with edges applied after the garment has been seamed. To do this, stitches must be picked up evenly along the edge, knitted in the stitch pattern given in the instructions and then cast off. Have the right side of the fabric facing you.

*Insert the needle from the back to the front, either under both loops at the top of cast off stitches, or between the loops of the first stitch in from the edge of the knitting. Wind the yarn round the point of the needle as when knitting a stitch and pull this loop through, leaving a stitch on the needle, (see Fig 18).

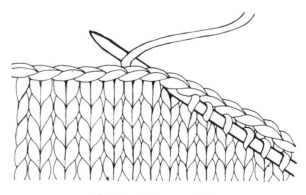

fig 18 picking up stitches

Continue working from the * in this way until the required number of stitches have been picked up, then complete the edge as given in the instructions.

137

More about knitting yarns

The craft of hand-knitting is used to produce an interlocking fabric with the aid of a pair of needles, suitable yarn and a pair of willing hands! The most important factor in this exercise is the yarn, which will have been chosen by the original designer as being most suitable for the garment she has in mind, then allied to the stitch pattern and needle size which will achieve the ideal fabric.

Choosing yarn

The days are long past when 'yarn' and 'wool' meant one and the same thing and the revival of interest in knitting has produced an enormous range of excellent yarns. Many people find this baffling; how do you choose? Can you substitute one yarn for another? Can you save money by buying a cheaper quality than the one specified in the instructions?

To a large extent the answers to these questions will depend on personal preference and circumstances. Many knitting enthusiasts shudder at the thought of using anything but pure wool; they like its unique texture and 'feel'. Others, who have to think about hard wear and the number of times a garment must go into the washing machine, will choose a yarn manufactured for this purpose, irrespective of fibre content. Some of the most beautiful yarns are also expensive and those on a limited budget will regretfully choose a cheaper product. Whatever your circumstances, it is worth inspecting and touching the yarn carefully before purchase, as this is one of the pleasures of hand-knitting.

Ply

You should beware of thinking that the term 'ply' denotes a yarn of a definite thickness. Yarn is made up of single, spun threads and it is the thickness or thinness of these spun threads which is defined in a system called 'yarn counting'. These in turn make up the 'ply' — two, three, four or more — which are then combined and twisted in many different ways to produce the finished product. A soft Shetland 2 ply can be thicker than a 4 ply and a standard double knitting quality can also be made from 4 plys.

The following ply classification is generally applicable to the majority of hand-knitting yarns available, whether produced from natural or man-made fibres, or combinations of both.

Baby yarns are usually made from the highest quality fibres, such as soft botany wool from around the neck of the Merino sheep. They are available in 2, 3 or 4 plys, also double knitting and chunky weights.

Baby quickerknit yarns are generally equivalent to a 4 ply but as they are very loosely twisted, they produce soft, lightweight yarns.

2, 3 and 4 ply yarns use combinations of many different fibres and are usually finer than double knitting weights.

Double knitting yarns again vary enormously in their composition but they are usually almost double the thickness of 4 ply yarns.

Chunky and double double knitting weights are extra thick yarns vary considerable in their construction — 'Aran' weights come into this classification.

Substituting yarns

It is always safest to use the yarn specified in your pattern. The design, texture, colours, tension and the amount needed will all have been carefully calculated on that product. It *is* possible to buy a substitute, if you really cannot obtain the brand specified, but you must experiment with tension samples until you achieve the exact tension given in the instructions. Don't expect the texture of the garment to look the same as that shown in the illustration and remember that the quantity given will vary.

The yarn spinners introduce new yarns each year into their range and withdraw older ones. This can cause problems if you keep a favourite pattern for some time and expect to find the original yarn still available. In this event, seek the help of your stockist who will be able to check the fibre content of the original yarn and suggest a substitute.

Colours in each range are also regularly appraised and changed, according to fashion trends, so it is not always possible to obtain the exact colours shown in an illustration.

Sources of supply

It is always safest to stick to the named yarn spinner and to purchase from their retailer. If something goes wrong you know who to approach. If you run out of yarn you stand the chance of being able to buy the odd ball in the same dye lot to complete a garment. You will be able to choose from an enormous range of colours, yarn types and fibres, as both knitting leaflets and magazine patterns usually specify the branded products from major spinners.

Many large chain stores stock their own range of yarns and these are sometimes a little cheaper than similar branded products. They are to a very high quality since they are made by the major spinners for the stores. If you can find the colour, type and fibre content to suit your purpose, this is a good way of cutting costs. However, the range of yarns is usually rather limited.

Mail order is a useful way of buying yarn, particularly if you are house-bound, or live in an area without much choice in local shops. The best firms offer a postal equivalent of the 'own brand' yarns described above, but branded yarns can also be

obtained from some suppliers. In these circumstances you must remember that the high cost of postage will add considerably to the price per ball. Mail order, however, is an excellent way of finding specialist yarns for experimental work; most craft magazines carry advertisements from specialist suppliers.

Most keen knitters will have occasionally bought supplies from a market stall. In the traditional textile manufacturing areas especially, markets will often have a tempting array of odd bundles of interesting yarn. A discerning and experienced knitter can often find true bargains this way, but there are risks too which must be taken into consideration. The fibre composition of the yarn is often unspecified, so you have no idea of pressing or aftercare procedure. You might be obliged to buy a set quantity which may turn out to be too little or too much. If the dye turns out to be unstable, or if each ball or hank contains an unacceptable number of knots, you have no way of reproaching the manufacturer.

One other point about cost; yarn is sold by weight, not length and this is governed by British Standard regulations. Inspect the ball band to see what weight you are buying. An apparently 'cheap' ball may only weigh 20 grams and gram for gram may actually be more expensive than a 25 gram ball costing a few pence more.

Aftercare of yarns

Time and skill have to be lavished on making hand-knitted garments but many people do not realise that pressing and laundering also demand special techniques. A beautifully knitted jersey may be ruined by clumsy washing or pressing.

The following suggestions will help to keep all your knitted garments in pristine condition:

1) Use a detergent or soap specially recommended for knitwear. This will dissolve easily and will not contain harmful bleach, more suitable for house-hold linens.

Adding some fabric conditioner to the final rinse also helps to keep the fibres smooth. Harsh detergents are particularly unsuitable for pure wool, as they remove the natural oiliness.

Beware of adding so much soap or detergent that it is difficult to remove during rinsing.

2) Never soak hand-knitted garments. Wash them frequently and keep the washing process brief.

3) Avoid rubbing — this can cause a permanently 'felted' effect.

4) If machine-washing, carefully follow the programme recommended by the manufacturers for knitwear. Also check the soap or detergent instructions.

5) Avoid very hot water.

6) Hand-wash by gently squeezing; don't lift the garment out of the water so that the weight distorts the shape.

7) Rinse very thoroughly, then gently squeeze out as much water as you can.

8) If spin-drying, carefully follow the programme recommended by the manufacturer.

9) To dry a garment pad a table with newspaper then cover this with a thick, white or colour-fast towel. Put the garment on this, patting it into shape and let it dry away from direct heat or sunlight.

You can also buy special 'frames' to fit over a bath.

10) For a final airing, a garment can be pegged from under the arms on a line — never peg from the shoulders.

Re-cycling of yarns

Nothing need ever be wasted in knitting! The interlocking structure of the stitches make it possible to unpick each section back from the casting off to the very beginning.

The secret lies in a little pre-planning when each garment is completed against the day when you may wish to re-use the yarn. So often the real problem lies in unpicking the seams which are difficult to see against the knitted fabric. It is very easy to snip the knitting rather than the seam.

To overcome this, when seaming the sections together use an odd length of brightly contrasting coloured yarn to run through a small section of the seaming stitches on the wrong side of the work. This will be invisible from the right side but will provide a clear guide to the actual seaming stitches.

When you have unpicked the seams, find the last fastened-off loop of each section and unravel this. You will now be able to pull out each row of knitting. It is best to wind the yarn into hanks as you unpick it, winding it round the back of a chair. If you wind it straight away into balls you run the risk of stretching the yarn.

The yarn will look crinkled but can easily be restored to a smooth finish by careful hand-washing. Hang each hank out to dry thoroughly, the rewind into *loose* balls and the yarn is ready to use again.

Acknowledgements

The publishers acknowledge with thanks the following, who have given permission for their photographs and engravings to be reproduced in this book: Ralph Kleinhempel GmbH & Co for 'The Knitting Madonna' – the altar piece of Buxtehude, painted by Meister Bertram of Menden, Germany circa 1400, shown on page 7; the Royal National Lifeboat Institution, West Quay Road, Poole, Dorset, for the photograph of an unknown lifeboatman shown on page 10; The Sutcliffe Gallery, Whitby, North Yorkshire, for the photograph of Harry Freeman shown on page 32; The National Museum of Ireland, Dublin, for the photograph of the spinning wheel from Belleek, Co. Fermanagh, shown on page 48; The Aberdeen University Library for the photograph of Shetlanders washing and dressing Shetland shawls, shown on page 68; The Shetland Museum and Library, Lerwick, for the photograph shown on page 82; The Mary Evans Picture Library, London, for the Iceland farm shown on page 108 and the view of Port Stanley Harbour, Falklands, shown on page 118.

The publishers would also like to thank World of Wicker, 16 St John's Road, Tunbridge Wells, for kindly lending them the cane chair shown on pages 91 and 131, and the basket shown on pages 3 and 20, John Hall for kindly lending them the model boat shown on pages 1, 9 and 139, and David and Jan Cundle for the loan of their horse Royal Swan shown on page 105.

All the models used in this book are non-professionals and the publishers thank the following people for giving their time to model the garments: Dexter Johnson, pages 14, 123; Elisabeth Pangarzi, pages 16, 29, 59; Paul Watkinson, page 21; Haydn Cole and Louise Bankes page 22; Victoria Martin, pages 26, 89; Helene Reinders, pages 37, 72, 93, 111; Jonathan Scotland, page 37; Dinah Wood, page 41; Sarah Cattell, page 45; Maarten Reinders, pages 53, 61, 111; Su Tuck, pages 54, 105; Ted and Gwen Watkinson, page 65; Rosalind Dace, page 76; Ian Gilmore, page 96; Martin de la Bedoyere, pages 98, 102; Kate Horgan, page 103; Ruth Saunders, page 115; Martha Ocampo, page 127, front and back cover; Christian Hore, back cover.

Spinners addresses

In case of difficulty in obtaining any of the yarns featured in this book, please write direct to the spinner concerned at the addresses given below, for details of your nearest stockist.

Emu yarns (UK)

Emu Wools Ltd.,
Consumer Services,
Leeds Road,
Greengates,
Bradford, BD10 9TE.

AUSTRALIA

Mr L Griffiths,
Karingal Vic/Tas Pty Ltd.,
6, Macro Court,
Rowville,
Victoria 3178.

CANADA

Ms Heather Patterson,
S.R. Kertzer Ltd.,
105A, Winges Road,
Woodbridge,
Toronto,
Ontario, L4L 6C2.

NEW ZEALAND

Mr L Griffiths,
Karingal Vic/Tas Pty Ltd.,
6, Macro Court,
Rowville,
Victoria 3178.

SOUTH AFRICA

Mr C Rayner,
Brasch Hobby,
P.O. Box 6405,
Johannesberg 2000.

USA

Mr R.W. Power Jnr.,
The Plymouth Yarn Co. Inc.,
P.O. Box 28,
500, Lafayette Street,
Bristol,
PA 19007.

Falkland Islands yarns (UK)

Ponytown Ltd.,
Lower Holme Mills,
Otley Road,
Baildon,
Shipley,
West Yorkshire, BD17 7LN.

Hayfield yarns (UK)

Hayfield Textiles Ltd.,
Glusburn,
Keighley,
West Yorkshire, BD20 8QP.

Jaeger yarns (UK)

Jaeger Handknitting Ltd.,
McMullen Road,
Darlington,
Co. Durham, DL1 1YD.

AUSTRALIA

All enquiries to:
Coats Patons Handknitting,
Thistle Street,
Launceston 7250
Tasmania.

NEW ZEALAND

Coats Patons (New Zealand) Ltd.,
263, Ti Rakan Drive,
Pakuranga,
Auckland.

USA

Susan Bates Inc.,
212, Middlesex Avenue,
Chester,
CT 06412.

Jamieson yarns (UK)

Jamieson Spinning Shetland Ltd.,
Jamieson Handknitting Ltd.,
93–95, Commercial Street,
Lerwick,
Shetland, ZE1 0BD.

Robin yarns (UK)

Robin Wools Ltd.,
Robin Mills,
Idle,
Bradford,
West Yorkshire, BD10 9TE.

AUSTRALIA

Karingal Vic/Tas Pty Ltd.,
6, Macro Court,
Rowville,
Victoria 3178

CANADA

S.R. Kertzer Ltd.,
105A Winges Road,
Woodbridge,
Toronto,
Ontario L4L 6C2

SOUTH AFRICA

Brasch Hobby,
P.O. Box 6405,
Johannesberg 2000.

USA

The Plymouth Yarn Co.,
P.O. Box 28,
500, Lafayette Street,
Bristol,
PA 19007

Scotnord yarns (UK)

Scotnord Yarns Ltd.,
P.O. Box 27,
Athey Street,
Macclesfield,
Cheshire, SK11 8EA.

AUSTRALIA

Scandic Import Company,
P.O. Box 120,
Vermont,
Victoria 3133.

USA

Reynolds Yarns Inc.,
15 Oser Avenue,
Hauppauge,
New York,
NY 11788.

Sunbeam yarns (UK)

Sunbeam Knitting Wools,
Crawshaw Mills,
Pudsey,
Leeds,
West Yorkshire, LS28 7BS.

USA

Tahki Imports,
11, Graphic Place,
Moonachie,
New Jersey 07074.

Wendy yarns (UK)

Carter & Parker Ltd,
Gordon Mills,
Guisley,
West Yorkshire, LS20 9PD.

AUSTRALIA

Craft Warehouse,
30, Guess Avenue,
Arncliffe,
New South Wales.

CANADA

White Buffalo Mills Ltd.,
545, Assiniboine Avenue,
Brandon,
Manitoba.

NEW ZEALAND

Wendy Wools (New Zealand) Ltd.,
P.O. Box 29107,
Greenwoods Corner,
Auckland.

Index

Book list

The following titles are recommended by the author for further reading.

Felkin, W. *History of machine-wrought hosiery and lace manufacturers* 1867. David & Charles, centenary edition, 1967.

Grass, M. and A. *Stockings for a queen.* Heinemann, 1967.

Hartley, M. and Ingilby, J. *The old hand-knitters of the Dales.* Dalesman Press, 1969.

Lloyd, T.H. *The English wool trade of the Middle Ages.* Cambridge University Press, 1977.

Thomas, M. *Knitting book.* Hodder & Stoughton, 1938. Reprinted by Dover Press.

Thomas, M. *Book of knitting patterns.* Hodder & Stoughton, 1943. Reprinted by Dover Press.

Thompson, G. *Patterns for Guernseys, Jerseys and Arans.* B.T. Batsford, 1969. Reprinted by Dover Press, 1971.

Weston, M. *The traditional sweater book.* Dorling Kindersley, 1986.

Wright, M. *Cornish guernseys and knit-frocks.* Ethnographica, 1979.